CASEBOOK

FOR

DATABASE PROCESSING:

FUNDAMENTALS, DESIGN, IMPLEMENTATION

FOURTH EDITION

David M. Kroenke

Theresa M. Kann

Macmillan Publishing Company
New York

Maxwell Macmillan Canada
Toronto

Maxwell Macmillan International
New York   Oxford   Singapore   Sydney

Executive Editor: Vernon R. Anthony
Developmental Editor: Peggy H. Jacobs
Production Editor: Constantina Geldis
Art Coordinator: Lorraine Woost
Cover Designer: Robert Vega
Production Buyer: Patricia A. Tonneman

Copyright © 1992 by Macmillan Publishing Company, a division of Macmillan, Inc.

Printed in the United States of America

All rights reserved. No part of this book may be reproduced or transmitted in any form or by any means, electronic or mechanical, including photocopy, recording, or any information storage and retrieval system, without permission in writing from the Publisher.

Macmillan Publishing Company
866 Third Avenue
New York, New York 10022

Macmillan Publishing Company is part of the
Maxwell Communication Group of Companies.

Maxwell Macmillan Canada, Inc.
1200 Eglinton Avenue East, Suite 200
Don Mills, Ontario M3C 3N1

Library of Congress Cataloging-in-Publication Data
Kroenke, David M.
    Casebook for Database processing: fundamentals, design,
implementation / David M. Kroenke, Theresa M. Kann.—4th ed.
    p.   cm.
    ISBN 0-02-366877-6
    1. Data base management.   I. Kann, Theresa.   II. Kann, Theresa.
Database processing. III. Title
QA76.9.D3K359 1992
005.74—dc20   91-36258
    CIP

Printing: 1 2 3 4 5 6 7 8 9   Year: 2 3 4 5

PREFACE

The Intended Audience for This Casebook
This Casebook is designed for use with the textbook *Database Processing*, 4th edition. It is written for students at the sophomore, junior, or senior level in both two- and four-year colleges and trade schools. It can be used by students in the classroom, in small study groups or for independent study. The system files and tables referred to in this text are available from your professor via his INSTRUCTOR'S DISK.

Why We Wrote This Casebook
We believe students prefer to practice career-oriented skills and techniques. This Casebook is a way for you to develop and practice the skills needed to design and implement a database processing system. The cases are examples of typical business situations. The questions following each case take you through each developmental process step-by-step. After working through the cases, you will have enough experience to apply the theory and techniques.

We feel that it is important for you to work with both of the current data models: Entity Relationships and Semantic Objects. This gives you the ability to compare the two models in similar situations.

The Design of This Casebook
We designed this Casebook to follow two different businesses through both the entity relationship and semantic object development processes. There are twelve cases in all. The first six cases and the last six cases are totally separate. Case 1 is an introduction to database processing using the Paradox database management system. Cases 2 through 6 are about the Northern Star Expeditions business. This is a skiing instruction and retail business whose owner, Lynn Lander, wants to develop a database processing system to support his marketing plan. Case 7 is an introduction to database processing similar to Case 1. Cases 8 through 12 are about the Skagit Valley Airplane Dealership business. A member of this family-owned business wants to franchise the dealerships.

The cases are presented so that you can work through the entire process with each business situation. The question format is the same for both cases. For example, the question format in Case 2 about Entity Relationship data modeling for the Northern Star Expeditions is the same as in Case 8 for the Skagit Valley Airplane Dealerships. We feel this approach has a major benefit for you. If you do both cases, you spend more time developing skills and less time understanding a set of instructions.

This Casebook uses the Paradox software to give examples of database processing implementation. It is NOT meant to be a tutorial for Paradox. You should work through the Paradox tutorials before attempting the Casebook material. Cases 1 and 7 supply you with tables and show you how to do simple queries. All of the instructions for the Paradox procedures are included in the text. In cases 6 and 12, you will create tables, a standard form, and a standard report. We don't want to overwhelm you with the possibilities Paradox offers. We only want you to understand the fundamentals of the implementation process.

We intentionally wrote this Casebook in a very conversational and supportive tone. It is meant to seem like an instructor is sitting beside you explaining each process. We want you not only to understand each step, but also to catch our fascination with and enthusiasm for database processing.

How To Use This Casebook
You can use this casebook to understand the Entity Relationship and/or the Semantic Object development process. The cases use the case studies as background knowledge and then describe a specific situation within the business. We make frequent references to the textbook to help you understand and coordinate the material. If you want to learn how to use the Entity Relationship model, do Cases, 2, 4, 8, and 10. Cases 3, 5, 9, and 11 explain the Semantic Object model. Cases 1, 6, 7, and 12 use the Paradox software and can be done with either model.

Cases 6 and 12 are partial implementations of previous cases, using the Paradox database management system. The implementation projects are very simple. To challenge yourself, you can try more complicated queries, forms, and reports to augment the ones presented in the cases.

We hope this casebook helps you understand and enjoy the skills needed to implement a database. Database processing will definitely be an exciting field for the 1990s. There will be many opportunities for you once you learn the skills in this casebook.

A NOTE TO INSTRUCTORS:

USE THIS FORM TO ORDER YOUR

INSTRUCTOR'S DISK FROM MACMILLAN.

HERE'S HOW IT WORKS ...

Just adopt **Database Processing: Fundamentals, Design, Implementation,** 4th edition, by David Kroenke or the **Casebook for Database Processing: Fundamentals, Design, Implementation,** 4th edition.

THEN, order the Instructor's Disk from Macmillan, which includes an electronic version of the text's transparencies, an ASCII version of the instructor's manual, and the data disks that accompany the Casebook.

To order your Instructor's Disk today, just contact your sales representative or Macmillan Faculty Support at 1-800-228-7854 ext. 3613. Tell them you would like to receive ISBN 002-366879-2.

CONTENTS

                                                                   Page

PART I: NORTHERN STAR EXPEDITIONS CASE STUDIES

Background Information for Cases 2, 3, 4, 5, and 6	10
Case 1 - Introduction to Database Processing	13
Case 2 - Entity-Relationship Modeling	23
Case 3 - Semantic Object Modeling	27
Case 4 - Transforming an Entity-Relationship Data Model into a Relational Database Design	35
Case 5 - Transforming a Semantic Object Data Model into a Relational Database Design	39
Case 6 - Partial Implementation of a Relational Database Design	43

PART II: SKAGIT VALLEY AIRPLANE DEALERSHIPS CASE STUDIES

Background Information for Cases 8, 9, 10, 11, and 12	48
Case 7 - Introduction to Database Processing	55
Case 8 - Entity Relationship Modeling	60
Case 9 - Semantic Object Modeling	63
Case 10 - Transforming an Entity Relationship Data Model into a Relational Database Design	70
Case 11 - Transforming a Semantic Object Model into a Relational Database Design	74
Case 12 - Partial Implementation of a Relational Database Design	78
STANDARD REPORTS	81
ANSWERS (Cases 2–6)	85

PART I

NORTHERN STAR EXPEDITIONS CASE STUDIES

BACKGROUND INFORMATION FOR CASES 2, 3, 4, 5, AND 6

Northern Star Expeditions is a fifteen-year-old company that offers cross-country skiing instruction and sponsors cross-country tours in the Cascade Mountain Range. It also sponsors backcountry expeditions in mountain ranges around the world. Northern Star is owned and managed by Lynn Lander.

Northern Star's business is highly seasonal. The first courses and tours begin in mid-October and the season is over by mid-April. During this period of time, Northern Star conducts twelve beginning ski courses, six intermediate ski courses, and one advanced backcountry expedition. Also, Northern Star operates eight tours over the winter.

Lynn likes to keep the staff very lean. He employs a secretary/office manager, cook/maintenance personnel, and a number of ski instructors and tour guides. The instructors and guides are paid a per-diem rate for the days they work. The instructors are all excellent skiers and can teach any of the courses. The tour guides trade off directing cross-country tours and pulling sleds that carry equipment and supplies for the courses and the tours. There are also a number of apprentice ski instructors who are unpaid but who receive room and board when they are helping with courses and tours. The cook/maintenance staff works in the base camp. In Lynn's simple filing system, he has a sheet for each employee with their name, social security number, address, city, state, zip code, and phone number. During the season he uses three-by-five-inch cards to keep track of which instructor, apprentice, or tour guide is on which job. On the card he writes the person's name, the number of the course or tour he or she is working, and the date. He revises the cards when people change jobs.

Beginning Ski Courses

The beginning ski course consists of five days of instruction followed by a four-day trip skiing hut-to-hut in the Cascade Mountains. The students live and eat at the lodge during the instructional phase. On the touring portion of the course, students stay in huts along groomed trails; food is provided and prepared by the Northern Star staff.

Each introductory course is limited to ten students. Except in unusual circumstances, such as not having enough snow to ski on, all the classes are within 90 percent of capacity.

Tour guides pull food and supplies to the huts on two sleds. The tour guides help the instructors set up the huts as well as serve as cooks. The introductory courses are staffed by two paid instructors, one unpaid apprentice instructor, and the two tour guides. Food and lodging are provided to all instructors, tour guides, and apprentices for both phases of the course.

Intermediate Ski Courses

The intermediate courses consist of five days of skiing on different slopes of two mountains. Students in these courses live in a rustic resort located near the mountains. All meals are provided by the resort. Food and lodging are provided by the resort to Northern Star on a fixed price-per-person contract basis. Northern Star includes the cost of food and lodging in the package price it offers its customers.

Intermediate courses are limited to eight students and are staffed by one paid instructor and one unpaid apprentice instructor. Again, both paid and unpaid instructors are provided lodging and food during the course.

Backcountry Expeditions

The backcountry expedition consists of a group of eight to ten advanced/expert skiers and two instructors. The duration and location of the expedition varies from year to year but generally involves a two-to-three week trip down a mountain on another continent. Participants meet in a departure city located in the United States and travel together to the base on the mountain. Food is provided for the planned number of days on the mountain. Hotels and transportation in the destination country are normally included in the course cost, although the specific policy depends on the country and varies from year to year. All travel, hotel, and food costs for the two instructors are paid by Northern Star. Lynn tries to plan these trips so that Northern Star nets about $3,500 on the trip after all direct expenses (not including overhead).

Northern Star rents all the necessary skiing equipment for introductory students. Intermediate and advanced students are expected to provide their own equipment. Northern Star will rent skis, boots, and poles to intermediate and advanced students, if necessary. Students are required to provide all personal clothing and camping equipment, including sleeping bags, tents, mattresses, and so on.

Cross-Country Tours

In addition to the skiing courses and expeditions, Northern Star operates eight five-day touring trips in the Cascade Mountains. The tours are a combination of trail and backcountry skiing. The first and the last nights are spent in huts and the middle two nights are spent snow camping. Each trip consists of six customers, two paid tour guides, and one apprentice tour guide who helps set up camp and cook meals.

Although the tours and skiing courses are separately operated, they are scheduled to be on the mountain at the same time so that, in an emergency, the ski and tour staff personnel could support one another. To facilitate cooperation between these trips, tour guides occasionally serve as apprentice ski instructors and ski instructors occasionally operate as tour guides.

Northern Star rents all necessary touring equipment to the customers. As with the ski classes, personal camping equipment and clothing is provided by customers.

The Ski Store

Northern Star operates a small skiing store in a shed adjacent to the lodge. It is a small-scale operation that grew out of the need to provide inexpensive but necessary items (sunscreen, retainers for eyeglasses, hats, gloves, etc.) to participants during the courses. Invariably, someone would forget such an item and ask one of the staff members to pick it up during a grocery shopping trip in town (twenty-seven miles away). Northern Star began offering such items for sale as a way of dealing with this irritating but real need.

Several years ago, a salesperson for one of the suppliers of the skiing equipment used in the introductory class introduced the idea to Lynn that Northern Star begin to sell skis, boots, poles, gaiters, jackets, sweaters, and other paraphernalia to attendees. Northern Star was buying such equipment at wholesales prices anyway, and the supplier suggested that Northern Star become a full-scale retail outlet.

Over the years, the operation has grown into a small sideline business. Lynn sells equipment at an average of 25 percent markup. He estimates he sells about $35,000 (retail prices) worth of equipment on direct expenses of about $20,000. Often Northern Star is not billed for the merchandise for a month to six weeks after it is received. In this time, Lynn hopes to sell a substantial portion of it. He rolls inventory that is unsold by the season's end into the equipment inventory for next year's beginning classes. Unfortunately, pilferage is a problem. He estimates that he loses 15 percent of his inventory to theft. One year he even lost a pair of skis to theft! Overall, Lynn thinks he nets about $20,000 on the store, not including overhead.

As with the rest of this business, record keeping is minimal. He verifies deliveries against purchase orders and checks invoices against sales orders. The office manager prepares checks to vendors. He keeps an informal inventory of items on hand and sold. Lynn would like to know which customer has bought what type of equipment. He's positive the retail business could be more profitable with some targeted marketing.

Overall, Lynn operates his business very informally. He has been in business for fifteen years and he knows about what to spend for each course on equipment, supplies, food, and other expenses. He also has an intuitive sense of his personnel costs. At the end of the year, he totals his revenue, subtracts expenses, and determines what he has earned. He hopes to clear around $65,000 before taxes for the year (this includes his salary). In the past five years, his actual profit has ranged from a low of $13,700 to a high of $87,500.

Lynn is not at all satisfied with this arrangement. He knows that his record keeping is minimal and that he runs his business literally by the seat of his pants. He senses there are opportunities for increasing his profit margin, but he never has time to develop a system that would help him do this. By the end of the season, he is usually so exhausted that he takes six weeks off. Then, he repairs Northern Star facilities and begins his marketing promotion for the coming year. There is never time to improve his record keeping, marketing, and financial management systems.

Lynn is satisfied with the effectiveness of marketing for the introductory ski courses and the tour trips. Each season he is able to fill almost all of the slots available, and he often has a waiting list. Northern Star cannot expand the size or the number of courses and trips, because the company cannot obtain more permits from the Forest Service to put more people on the mountain.

Lynn is not at all satisfied with the marketing for the intermediate and expedition courses, however. He believes that he has a marketing gold mine in the customers who have completed the basic course. When he has the time to call one of these customers, he is almost always able to sell them an intermediate course. It's as if the customers are waiting to be called, to be reminded of the good experience they had, and to enroll in another class.

In spite of this opportunity, Northern Star does almost nothing with the list of prior students. In some years, he is able to send out a few Christmas cards, but this is done informally and without regard to any marketing strategy.

CASE 1
INTRODUCTION TO DATABASE PROCESSING

The textbook, *Database Processing: Fundamentals, Design, Implementation*, fourth edition, contains a robust and comprehensive process for developing databases and their applications. This process is effective for designing and implementing very large and complicated databases. Because it is a robust process you will need to learn a number of complicated concepts and techniques before you will have an opportunity to work with an actual database. This could be frustrating for you; you may not be able to see the relevance of the conceptual material if you have no database processing experience at all.

To reduce the risk of such frustration, this case study introduces you to database processing. The purpose of this case study is twofold: to give you a chance to work through the tutorial for the specific database management system you will be using and to examine sample tables in Paradox.

Specifically, you will:
- Become familiar with the facilities at your school for database processing.
- Work through the tutorial for the specific database management system you will be using.
- If you will be using Paradox, you will retrieve information from the sample tables that are on the floppy disk provided with the casebook. This process is called querying the database.

The time you will need to complete this case can vary greatly. Working through this case could take you as little as fifteen minutes if you already know Paradox. But for many of you it could take up to four hours, since you'll need to learn how to use your school's computer laboratory, work through the tutorials, and then complete the questions about the sample tables on the disk.

Steps to become familiar with your school's database processing facilities:
1. Locate the computer laboratory and the specific machines that have a database management system installed on them. If you have questions about getting started, ask the class instructor, the teaching assistant, or the computer laboratory assistant.

2. It's important to thoroughly understand the database management system you will be using by doing the tutorials. Again, if you have questions about getting started, ask the class instructor, the teaching assistant, or the computer laboratory assistant.

3. If you are using Paradox, you can now go on to completing the questions about the sample tables. The questions assume you have worked through the tutorials and have the Paradox, instructional manuals available in case you need to review specific commands.

4. If you are not using Paradox, you can go on to Case 2.

In this case study you will pretend you are in the middle of a job search. You have already narrowed your career fields to Information Systems Specialist, Human Resource Specialist, and Accountant. Now you want specific information about the type of job and the company. Suppose you could go to the placement center and look up this information in an automated database.

We created the design for the Job Search Database without regard to which software package we'd use to implement it. This is called a Database Management System (DBMS) independent design. We then transformed it to a DBMS dependent design. The word "dependent" means dependent on the software package; in this case, Paradox. It's important to remember that designing a database is a generic process and implementation is specific to the DBMS.

Questions for Querying Sample Tables
To get started, look at each of the sample tables. By examining the data tables, you will begin to understand their structure. There are two tables that are used in this case. Each table begins with C1, for Case 1. The first sample table, C1-Job, contains information on the job number, job title and description, salary, and corresponding company number. The second sample table, C1-Com, contains the company information. This information includes the company number, a business description, the number of employees, the annual revenue, and whether it is an international company. You might have noticed that both C1-Job and C1-Com have a company number in the tables. This is how the tables are related to each other. You will see why these relationships between the tables are important as you work through the following questions.

To complete the following questions, you will examine the sample tables and then do three queries on the tables. Querying is an excellent way to begin to understand a database design. This means you give the DBMS specific directions to retrieve and present the information you want. At the placement center you would query the Job Search Database. Querying a database is fun because of the possibilities and also frustrating because of the limitations of the DBMS.

The following commands are for your easy reference:

FREQUENTLY USED COMMANDS IN PARADOX
F1 - Help
F2 - Do-It!, Perform or end an operation
F3 - Up one image
F4 - Down one image
F5 - Enter an example element for multitable queries
ALT F5 - Edit in a field
F6 - Place checkmark in column for a query
ALT F7 - Generate standard report
ALT F8 - Clear the workspace
F10 - Display menu
F10|View|Enter|Use arrow keys to move to table name|Enter - To see the table
F10|Tools|Rename|Use arrow keys to move to table name|Type new table name|Enter - To rename a table
F10|Ask|Enter|Use arrow keys to move to table name|Enter - To create a query table

---

In questions 5–11 you examine the structure of the sample tables and the data in the sample tables, do two single-table queries and one linked-table query. In question 5 you will examine the structure of table C1-Job. In question 6 you will examine the structure of table C1-Com. For questions 7 and 8 you will examine the data in C1-Job and C1-Com, respectively. You will do a query by selecting specific fields in the table C1-Job for question 9 and do a query using a wild card operator on table C1-Job in question 10. The last question asks you to do a query on the linked tables of C1-Job and C1-Com. The answers for this case will be the tables you generate from the queries. They will be named C1-1, C1-2, and C1-3. For each question we give the Paradox commands in bold letters.

5. For this question you will look at the table structure of C1-Job. First, you need to tell Paradox where the table is. After starting the Paradox program, insert the casebook diskette in drive A.

Case 1 - Introduction to Database Processing 15

These are the commands to tell Paradox that the table is on the diskette in drive A.

> Tools|More|Directory|(Delete the existing directory with the backspace key) Type a:|Enter|**Right Arrow (OK)|Enter.**

In the lower right-hand corner you will see the message "The working directory is now a:\."

Now you can look at the structure of C1-Job. The structure defines the data requirements for each field. These are the commands to bring up the structure table for C1-Job.

> Tools|Info|Structure|Enter|Use arrow keys to select the table name|Enter.

Look at each field data requirement to see if it is an alphanumeric field, numeric field, or date field. If it's an alphanumeric field, notice how many characters are allowed. Notice which fields are keyed. They have an asterisk in the field type column. When you are done, use **ALT F8** to clear the workspace.

> Alt F8

6. Now you can look at the structure of C1-Com.

> Tools|Info|Structure|Enter|Use arrow keys to select the table name|Enter.

Look at each field data requirement to see if it is an alphanumeric field, numeric field, or date field. If it's an alphanumeric field, notice how many characters are allowed. When you are done, use **ALT F8** to clear the workspace.

> Alt F8

7. Now that you know the structure of the C1-Job table, you will look at the data in the table.

> View|Enter|Use arrow keys to select C1-Job|Enter

The table will appear as the first image on the screen. You saw the fields of Job Description and Salary in the structure table, but you don't see them on the screen. By pressing the right arrow key, you will be able to see the other fields. Review the data in each field, so you are familiar with it before you start doing queries.

> Press Right Arrow key five times to see the other fields.
> Press Right Arrow to return to the first column.

8. Examine the data in table C1-Com while the C1-Job table is still on the screen.

> **F10|View|Enter|Use arrow keys to select C1-Com|Enter**

C1-Com will appear as the second image on the screen. Review the data in each field, so you are familiar with it before you start doing queries.

> Press Right Arrow key five times to see the other fields.
> Press Right Arrow to return to the first column.

Clear the screen.

> **Alt F8**

9. A powerful aspect of database processing is the ability to query the database. This is the first query on a single table. For this query you will answer the question, "What are the job titles and job descriptions in the C1-Job table?"

    Paradox uses a method called query by example. This means you create a query table that looks like an example of the answer table you want. To select fields to appear in the answer table, move to each field and press **F6**. F6 is a toggle key: use it to place and delete checkmarks in the query tables.

    These are the commands to build a query on the C1-Job table to answer the question:

> **Ask|Enter|Use arrow keys to move to C1-Job|Enter**
> **Right Arrow|Right Arrow|Right Arrow| F6, Right Arrow, F6**

You have created the query table. The checkmarks represent the fields that will be in the

Case 1 - Introduction to Database Processing

answer table.

Now execute the query with the Do-It! key.

> **F2**

Answer tables are only temporary tables. When you create the next answer table, this will be deleted, so you must rename it to save it. Rename it C1-1.

> **F10|Tools|Enter (Rename)|Enter (Table)|Enter|Enter (Selecting Answer)|Type A:C1-1**

The table will reappear with C1-1 in the left-most column.

Clear the screen.

> **Alt F8**

10. For the next query determine the job numbers for the Human Resource Specialist jobs. Display the job numbers and the Human Resource Specialist job title.

    The first step is to create a query table for C1-Job like you did in Question 9.

    > **Ask|Enter|Use arrow keys to move to C1-Job|Enter**

    Now you want to indicate that the Job# field and the Job Title will be in the answer table. While you're in the Job Title field, you want to indicate that you want only the Human Resource Specialist titles. You can type Human Resource Specialist, but that is a lot of typing; instead use the wild card operator (..). Type **H..** beside the checkmark.

> **Right Arrow|F6|Right Arrow|Right Arrow|F6|Type H.. beside the checkmark|F2**

Since Answer tables are temporary tables, you need to rename the table C1-2.

> **F10|Tools|Enter (Rename)|Enter (Table)|Enter|Enter (Selecting Answer)|Type A:C1-2**

Clear the screen for the last query.

> **Alt F8**

11. The last query uses linked tables. Linked tables are necessary when the answer to the question requires information from two or more tables. Querying from linked tables is similar to querying from one table, except that you fill out a query by example for each table, and you use example elements to tell Paradox how the tables are linked. Linking tables is an important part of database design. You will learn about it in the upcoming textbook chapters and cases.

    For this query answer the question, "What are the business descriptions for each job title?"

    The answer table for this query consists of the Job Title field in the C1-Job table and the Business Description field in the C1-Com table. These are the commands for setting up the linked tables:

> **Ask|Enter|Use arrow keys to move to C1-Job|Enter**
> **Right Arrow|Right Arrow|F5|Type e (for example element)|Right Arrow|F6**

You have done the query by example for the first table. Now you need to add the second table to the query, link it to the first, and designate which fields you want displayed.

> **F10|Ask|Enter|Use arrow keys to move to C1-Com|Enter**
> **Right Arrow|F5|Type e|Right Arrow|F6|F2**

Rename the Answer table C1-3.

> **F10|Tools|Enter (Rename)|Enter (Table)|Enter|Enter (Selecting Answer)|Type A:C1-3.**

You are now familiar with Paradox. As you work through Cases 2, 3, 4, and 5, you will learn how to design a database. In Case 6 you will use Paradox again to implement a part of your design.

CASE STUDIES FOR

NORTHERN STAR EXPEDITIONS

CASE 2
ENTITY-RELATIONSHIP MODELING

Learning Objectives

The purpose of this case is to interpret a user's requirements for a database processing system and to build the user's data model. This will fulfill a major portion of the requirements phase of the database development tasks. In this case Lynn Lander wants to create a marketing plan for his ski instruction business. Specifically, in this case you will:

- Develop a data model that represents part of the data model Lynn has of his business and the marketing plan he wants to create.
- Identify the entities in the data model.
- Identify the properties of the entities.
- Define the domains of the properties.
- Represent the relationships between the entities.
- Create a diagram for the data model.

Questions for Creating an Entity-Relationship (E-R) Model

The questions for this case are split into two parts. In Part 1 you will create different types of entities and appropriate property lists from the Northern Star Expeditions case study. In Part 2 you will create an E-R diagram.

While you are answering these questions, remember that Lynn has a mental picture of a data structure for his business. You will be modeling his data model. In other words, he knows what is important to him in his work environment and the relationships between these things. It's your job to represent what's important to him in entities and properties and then represent the relationships in an E-R diagram. Try to adopt his vantage point as you answer the following:

Part 1

1. The first step in developing an E-R model is to identify the entity classes, which are collections of entities of the same type. Entity classes will be referred to as entities from here on. Entities are usually represented by nouns in the case study. They are written in all capitals.

    (a) Reread the case study and identify at least ten possible entities in Lynn's work environment. When Lynn thinks of his business, he certainly thinks of customers and employees. Lynn probably doesn't think of different types of customers, so the entity is CUSTOMER. However, there are different types of employees. The entities could be EMPLOYEE, INSTRUCTOR, OFFICE MANAGER, and COOK/MAINTENANCE PERSON. Use these examples and determine five other entities. Remember that data modeling is as much art as it is science. The entities you choose may not be the same ones your classmates choose.

2. Each entity has properties, or, as they are sometimes called, attributes, that describe entity characteristics. An identifier is a property that uniquely identifies an object. An example is the social security number for an employee. Many people have the same name, but each person has a unique social security number. The properties may be single- or multiple-valued.

    (a) Choose three of your entities and create a property list for them. Put the identifier as the first property and underline it. Some of the properties you will find in the case study, but others you will have to infer. For instance, Lynn does not mention how he will uniquely identify customers, so you could infer an identifier such as customer number. This is an example for the entity EQUIPMENT.

EQUIPMENT
Equipment #
Serial #
Equipment Name
Model
Size
Purchase Date
Manufacturer
Class MV

3. In the previous question you created property lists for three entities. Use those property lists to create instances for each of the entities. An instance is the representation of a particular entity. This is an instance of the entity EQUIPMENT:

Equipment #500
Serial #134QB7100
Touring Skis
Easy Glide
175 cm
June 15, 1991
Nordic Enterprises
Beginning Skiing, Tours

4. Relationships are the way entities are associated with one another. The number of entities in the relationship is the degree of the relationship.
   (a) Name the three fundamental types of binary relationships.

5. (a) Give an example of each type of binary relationship using the entities you listed in Question #1. If all of the relationships are not represented, then make up plausible examples so that you have an example of every type.
   (b) Are your examples HAS-A or IS-A relationships?

6. (a) The E-R Model defines a special type of entity called a weak entity. What is the definition of a weak entity?
   (b) What is a subclass of weak entities?
   (c) Look at your list of entities in Question #1. Are any of them weak entities? If so, name the entity it is dependent on and the type of weak entity it is.
   (d) If none of your entities are weak entities, make up a plausible example of both weak entities.

7. (a) What are generalization hierarchies?
   (b) In the case study, the entities EMPLOYEE and INSTRUCTOR fit this description. Name the supertypes and subtypes. (Hint: A supertype can be a subtype of another entity.)

8. (a) What are recursive relationships?
   (b) Pick an entity from Question #1 or make up one that represents a recursive relationship. Describe the situation that would create this relationship.

Case 2 - Entity-Relationship Modeling

Part 2
There are specific conventions for drawing an E-R diagram. Figure 1 is an example of an E-R diagram that is similar to the one you will be creating.

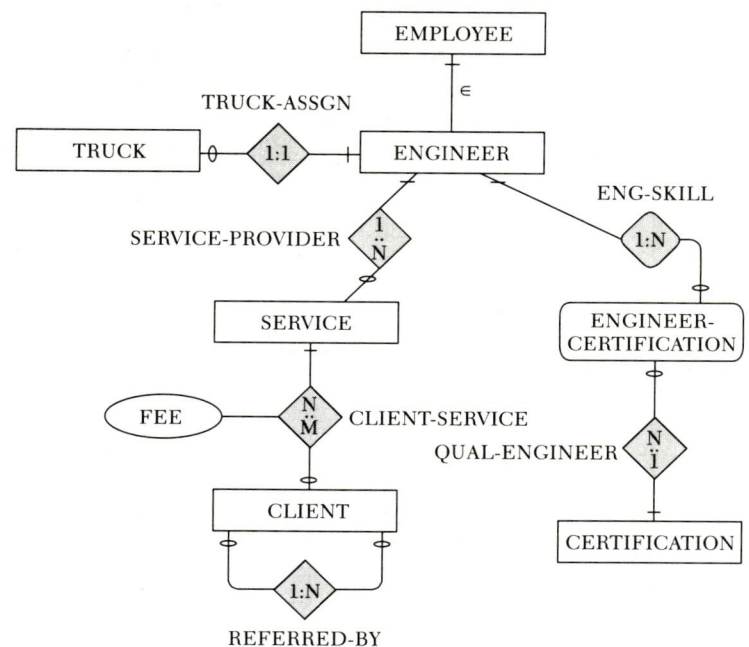

FIGURE 1
Example of entity-relationship diagram

9. Two special cases of entities are EMPLOYEE and INSTRUCTOR.
   (a) Diagram the relationship between EMPLOYEE, INSTRUCTOR, and their subtypes. Decide from the case study or make an assumption whether or not the relationships are exclusive and/or required. Show this in your diagram.

10. The INSTRUCTOR subtypes have relationships with the courses and trips.
    (a) Sketch the relationships between the instructors and the courses and trips showing the minimum and maximum cardinality that can be involved. The specific numbers of instructors, courses, and customers are in the case study. Name the relationships.

11. Sketch the CUSTOMER entity showing its minimum and maximum cardinality and relationship to the courses and tours. These relationships have the same relationship name, customer list, so it can be omitted.

12. Assume Lynn has specified an entity, CONTACT. This entity represents the contacts Lynn makes with each customer. The contact is with a specific customer and only after that customer's information is in the database.
    (a) What type of entity is CONTACT?
    (b) Diagram the relationship between CUSTOMER and CONTACT. Show the minimum and maximum entities involved and name the relationship.

13. Decide which entities are needed to represent the retail business and the equipment rental part of the business.

14. You now have four partial diagrams of the E-R model. Complete your E-R model by connecting the partial diagrams of EMPLOYEE, INSTRUCTOR, COURSE, CUSTOMER, and CONTACT. Add relationship diagrams for the entities in the retail and equipment rental part of the business. Omit the relationship names, since they make a completed diagram difficult to read.

15. Once the data model has been developed, the designer should consider the possibility of processing restrictions against the entities. Identify an entity that would have a restriction on (a) additions, (b) changes, and (c) deletions. Answer a, b, and c as if you were adding documentation to the E-R Diagram. Include the entity name, the type of restriction, and the correct procedure. This is an example for OFFICE MANAGER:

    OFFICE MANAGER
    Additions Processing Restriction
    Before OFFICE MANAGER data can be added, EMPLOYEE data must be added

16. E-R models should be evaluated once they are completed. Designers need to ask the questions: "Does this model accurately reflect the users' perceptions and mental models of their activity? Will it help the users respond consistently and successfully to one another and to their clients?" Think of three questions Lynn might ask that could be answered from the data model. Explain how your model answers these queries.

CASE 3
SEMANTIC OBJECT MODELING

Learning Objectives
The purpose of this case study is to interpret a user's requirements for a database processing system and to build the user's data model. Specifically, in this case you will:

- Develop a data model that accurately represents the data model Lynn has of his business.
- Identify the objects in the data model.
- Identify the properties of the objects.
- Represent the relationships between the objects.
- Create a diagram for the data model.

The major goal for the database development during the requirements phase is to build a data model that documents the things that are to be represented in the database, to determine the characteristics of those things that need to be stored, and to determine the relationships among them. The following questions will guide you in developing a semantic object data model.

A semantic object is one that models, in part, the meaning of the users' data. A semantic object (referred to as an object) is a named collection of properties that sufficiently describes a distinct identity. Objects are shown in portrait-oriented rectangles. The name of the object appears above or beneath the rectangle. Properties are written inside the rectangle. These diagrams are used by development teams to summarize the structure of objects and to present those structures visually.

You will use a bottom-up approach to develop this data model. You'll examine the application interface: the screens needed to input data for the Northern Star Expedition business. Then you'll work backwards, or reverse engineer, to derive the object structure. This approach is based on the theory that if you know how the users view their interface to the system, you can figure out what must be stored in the database.

The purpose of this case study is twofold. In Part 1 you will develop a set of objects from a set of screens, and in Part 2 you will have the opportunity to develop the remaining types of objects from additional screens. This will not be a comprehensive data model of the Northern Star Expedition business. When you finish, you will know how to develop a complete data model and can do that at a later date.

Part 1
Lynn wants to keep better track of the equipment used in the Beginning Ski Course. The courses run concurrently during the season (one during the week, one on Saturday, and one on Sunday). The ski instructors, apprentices, and tour guides are issued equipment for the season but not for their exclusive use. The equipment is issued to several instructors, apprentices, tour guides, and students, since the courses run concurrently. The information system consultant working with Lynn developed a set of prototype screens to track the equipment usage.

1. This is the first screen of the set:

```
                    COURSE INFORMATION

Course #:              Course Name:

Beginning Date:
End Date:
Day:

INSTR#           INSTRUCTOR         ADDRESS              PHONE

(Example)
482804920        Julie Adams        808 Lilly Lane       578-2389
```

(a) What object does this screen seem to be about? The title is usually a good indicator of an underlying object.

(b) What data is entered about the courses? Remember, an object is the representation of an important entity in the users' work environment—if Lynn wants information on instructors, then instructors is an object. (Note: For Part 1 questions, consider instructors, apprentices, and tour guides as instructors.) What is the relationship between the two objects?

(c) Diagram both objects. Each object has properties shown on the screen, but this is only the first screen. Following screens may show more properties for these objects. For your first draft of the object diagrams, it's convenient to put the name of the object at the top and draw a rectangle without a bottom line. This way you can list the properties as you find them. For your final diagram you will recopy the diagrams putting the non-object properties at the top, the object properties below them, and the composite groups last. The object names are placed below the rectangles.

Example of developing diagrams:

```
   INSTRUCTOR
|----------------------|
|Instructor #          |
|Name                  |
|Address               |
|Phone                 |
|                      |
```

Case 3 - Semantic Object Modeling

2. This screen would be used when the instructors are checking out equipment at the beginning of the season. A separate screen would be used for each instructor.

```
┌─────────────────────────────────────────────────────────────┐
│           EQUIPMENT CHECKOUT LIST FOR INSTRUCTORS           │
│                                                             │
│   INSTR NAME:                      INSTR #:                 │
│                                                             │
│   EQUIP#         EQUIPMENT DESCRIPTION         CONDITION    │
│                                                             │
└─────────────────────────────────────────────────────────────┘
```

   (a) What is the relationship between an instructor and the equipment checked out to him or her?

   (b) Update the INSTRUCTOR object to show its relationship to EQUIPMENT.

   (c) Create a new object: EQUIPMENT. Will this new object have INSTRUCTOR in it? How can you tell from the screen?

3. The beginning ski course is split into two parts: a large group demonstration and small group practice sessions. Each instructor is assigned a small group. Lynn wants to keep track of which student is assigned to which instructor. After the first class meeting, the instructors could enter the information on this screen:

```
┌─────────────────────────────────────────────────────────────┐
│                    BEGINNING SKI COURSE                     │
│           SMALL GROUP STUDENT LIST FOR INSTRUCTORS          │
│                                                             │
│   INSTR NAME:                      INSTR #:                 │
│                                                             │
│   STUDENT #    STUDENT NAME         ADDRESS         PHONE   │
│                                                             │
└─────────────────────────────────────────────────────────────┘
```

   (a) How is this screen similar to the screen in question #2?

   (b) Update INSTRUCTOR and create a new object as you did in Question #2.

4. This screen will show who has been assigned which equipment. The screen is grouped by equipment number and description and then by either instructor or student.

```
                    EQUIPMENT ASSIGNMENTS
    EQUIPMENT #:                    DESCRIPTION:

                    Instructor Assignments

    Instr #:                        Instr Name:

    (Example)
    489038729                       Julie Adams
    789302578                       Tom Gurrula

                    Student Assignments

    Student #:                      Student Name:

    (Example)
    690820937                       Cai Shuda
    589039483                       Amy Cyncenski
```

```
    EQUIPMENT #:                    DESCRIPTION:

                    Instructor Assignments

    Instr #:                        Instr Name:

                    Student Assignments

    Student #:                      Student Name:
```

(a) How many students and instructors can one piece of equipment be associated with?

(b) Update your EQUIPMENT object.

(c) Update your STUDENT object.

5. The final screen in the set is shown below. This screen lists students' names sorted in alphabetical order with their addresses and phone numbers.

Case 3 - Semantic Object Modeling

```
                    Beginning Ski Course
                    Directory # 91-103
                    December 1, 1991

STUDENT              ADDRESS                           PHONE

Chandler, Kevin      360 Oceanside Dr.                 789-3748
Edinburgh, Colyn     890 Seaside Street                783-5893
Gadfly, Gary         872 Pond Place                    784-4728
```

(a) This screen isn't meant to give you information about an individual student. It gives you information about a group of students: information about the course's student list. What is the underlying object?

(b) What are the four properties shown for the object?

(c) Diagram this object.

6. You now have all of the objects diagramed for this set of screens. Look over the screens and the objects to check for omissions and/or correct relationships. Redraw your objects as explained in Question #1.

You have successfully developed a small semantic object data model. This completes the major portion of the requirements stage of the database design project for this set of screens.

Part 2

In Part 1 you developed objects that supported the screens. There are other types of objects than the ones that you developed. In Part 2 you will develop diagrams for each type of object.

7. What type of objects did you develop in Part 1? Why do you think the objects were similar?

8. When a customer comes to the Northern Star Lodge, they often ask about a specific trail's difficulty and condition. Lynn wants this information on one screen. This is the prototype screen:

```
                        TRAIL INFORMATION

Trail Name:
Skill Level:
Total Length:
Total Elevation Gain:
Grooming Status:
Description:
```

(a) What type of object would represent this screen? What are two characteristics of the properties that support your claim?

(b) Diagram the object.

9. During the season Lynn offers his customers package deals on the retail ski equipment. Each package has a unique name and many choices of equipment features. When a customer asks about a package, one of Lynn's employees could use this screen to answer the question or take the order:

```
                        PACKAGE DEALS

Package Name:        HiCountry Explorer

Item Description:    XGL100 Skis

Feature Choice:      3/4 Metal Edge         $ 415.00
                     Full Metal Edge        $ 485.00
                     Item subtotal:         ($415.00)

Item Description:    Maketa Boots

Feature Choice:      Non-Insulated          $ 125.00
                     Insulated              $ 175.00
                     Item subtotal:

Item description:    Nvoget Poles

Feature Choice:      Standard               $ 125.00
                     Telescoping            $ 175.00
                     Item Subtotal:

Subtotal:
Tax:
Total Order:
```

(a) What are the single-valued properties of the PACKAGE object?

(b) What are the multivalued properties?

(c) What type of object is PACKAGE?

(d) Diagram the object.

10. The objects in Part 1 were all compound objects. How many subtypes of compound objects are there? Which subtypes are represented in the data model of Part 1?

11. Lynn has had many customers request private lessons. He asked the consultant to include a prototype screen for the information he needed. The screen looks like this:

Case 3 - Semantic Object Modeling

```
                    PRIVATE LESSON INFORMATION

   Lesson #:           Date:            Time:           Fee:

   Instructor #:    Name:
                    Address:
                    Phone:
                    Private Lesson Schedule:

   Student #:       Name:
                    Address:
                    Phone:
                    Current and Past Instructors:
```

(a) What special type of compound object is described above?
(b) Diagram the objects using at least three non-object properties. Show the relationship between the private lesson, the instructors, and the students.

12. The resort that Lynn contracts with for the intermediate courses sends Lynn an invoice after each course. The resort itemizes the bill by course and then by student service fees. The invoice form looks like this:

```
                    Glide On In Resort Invoice

   Invoice #:
   Invoice Date:

   Course Name:
   Course #:

   Student Name:
   Service Description:
   Service Fee:

   Service Description:
   Service Fee:
   (Example of repeating lines.)

   Student Name:
   Service Description:
   Service Fee:

   Subtotal:
   Tax:
   Total:
```

(a) Some of these properties you have seen before in other objects. That means this object will have object properties. What type of object is it?
(b) Diagram the object.
(c) Because this object is complicated, you will need to check whether you have shown the relationships correctly. Do this by diagraming the object; then, by looking at the object, create a form with instance properties (names and prices). Check to see if your form is the same as the one above.
(d) Create the RESORT INVOICE object specification and domain definitions for the single-valued properties not in objects. You will need to infer some domains. Follow the standards listed in the textbook in Figure 5–18.

13. Assume the object INSTRUCTOR is a generalization hierarchy with subtypes of SKI INSTRUCTOR, APPRENTICE, and TOUR GUIDE. The positions are mutually exclusive. Diagram INSTRUCTOR, including differing properties for the subtypes.

You have now developed every type of object that you can use in a data model.

CASE 4
TRANSFORMING AN ENTITY-RELATIONSHIP DATA MODEL INTO A RELATIONAL DATABASE DESIGN

In this case you will be given an Entity Relationship (E-R) data model for Lynn's marketing plan and then will transform it into a relational database design. In Case 11 you will implement a part of the database design.

The data model is a representation of the user's view of the data. The database design is a representation of the computer's view of the data. The database design is expressed as a DBMS-independent description of the data that is to be stored in the database, the relationships among the data, and the data constraints. Keeping the description independent of particular DBMS structures ensures that the design is determined only by user requirements and not by peculiarities or limitations of the DBMS to be used.

You will use another model, the relational model, to develop a DBMS-independent database design. In order to successfully transform the E-R model into a relational database design, you will need to know the normalization criteria covered in Chapter 6 of the text and the techniques for transforming data models into DBMS-independent designs covered in Chapter 7.

Specifically, in this part of the case study you will:
- Establish a relation for each entity
- Designate keys for each relation
- Evaluate each relation for normalization criteria
- Express the three types of binary and recursive relationships in terms of relations
- Complete the data structure design

Lynn Lander, the owner and manager of Northern Star Expeditions, felt he was missing many opportunities with his growing business, so he bit the bullet and hired a marketing consultant. The consultant observed Lynn's business during the last month of the season and then prepared a plan with Lynn during the two weeks after the season closed. Lynn wanted to get the plan done so that he could have an information systems consultant do the data model and the database design and implementation before the start of the next season.

Lynn had a multitude of ideas he had toyed with over the years. The consultant helped him focus on the three most promising areas: create a targeted mailing plan, develop ties with the nearby downhill ski operators, and start a series of activities for families. The consultant then wrote a plan that detailed Lynn's specifications in each area.

The targeted mailing plan had three parts. First, Lynn wanted to send registration slips to customers for the next class for which they were eligible. In order to do this, Lynn wanted to keep track of when each customer took each course. The second part was to send upgrade flyers to customers who had bought certain types of equipment. And finally, Lynn wanted to send out tailored evaluation/response survey forms to obtain feedback on his business and referrals. He decided to send everyone who responded a free rental coupon to show his appreciation.

Lynn had two purposes for developing ties with the local ski lift operators. He wanted to sell discounted season lift tickets at the lodge as a service to his customers. For his and the lift operator's records, he needed to match customers with the pass numbers they purchased. He also wanted to teach telemark lessons on the ski slopes. Telemarking is a skiing technique similar to downhill skiing except using cross-country skis. Lynn wanted to offer telemarking as a new class. In order to do this, he wanted to use the groomed slopes with chair lifts at the downhill ski resorts. Telemark lessons would prepare more of his students for the expeditions.

Lynn's third area of focus was family activities. He knew by the nation's demographics that there would be a mini baby boom in the 1990s. He wanted to make it easy for families with young children to ski together. This way the parents continue to be customers and the children become future customers.

Two of Lynn's experienced ski instructors were married and had two toddlers. They were interested in developing and supervising the program. For the first season they wanted to issue family plan passes, which were good for discounts on ski lessons and rental equipment. One customer could buy one family pass. They wanted to expand the program to include all-day activities for the children and youth racing.

Lynn was excited about his new marketing plan. He could encourage his customers to progress to the next level of skiing through the targeted mailing list. By adding a telemark class and selling season lift tickets, he had a class for each type of skier. And he could cater to the growing portion of his customers who have families.

Questions for Transforming the E-R Model Presented in Figure 1 into a Relational Database Design

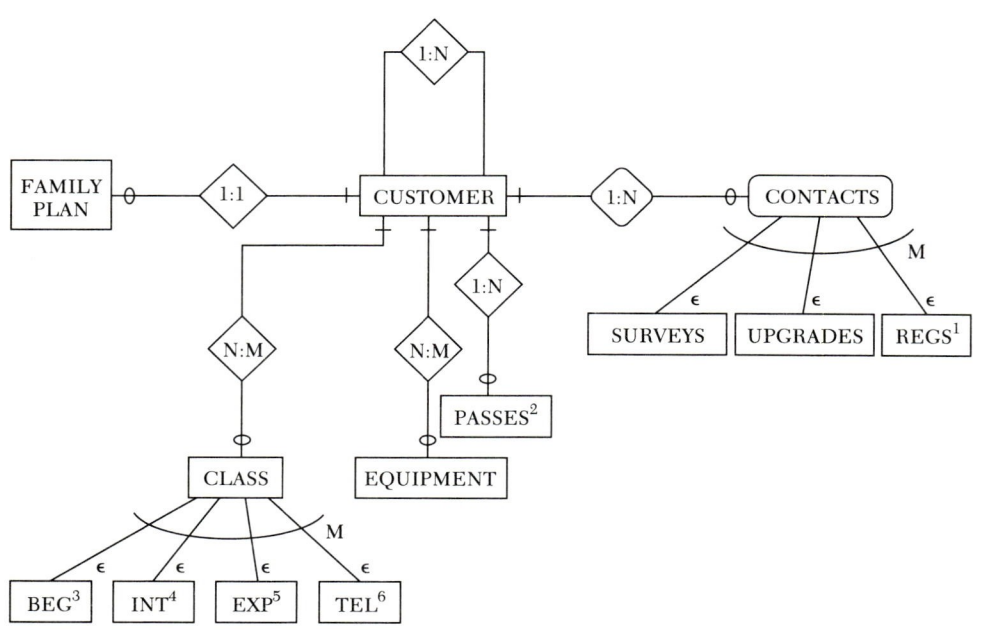

1. Registration slips
2. Discounted season lift passes
3. Beginning ski course
4. Intermediate ski course
5. Expeditions
6. Telemark Course

FIGURE 1

Case 4 - Transforming E-R Models 37

Before you begin the transformation process, carefully compare the description of Lynn's marketing plan to the data model. Make sure you understand how each part of the plan is represented in the model.

1. In general, the representation of entities with the relational model is straightforward. You begin by defining a relation for each entity. The name of the relation is the name of the entity, and the attributes of the relation are the properties of the entity. The property that identifies an entity becomes the key of the relation.

    (a) For each of the entities, create a relation that has a key and two attributes. Assume the key and attributes are single-valued. An example is the relation FAMILY PLAN:

    Relation Representing FAMILY PLAN Entity

    FAMILY PLAN (*Plan #*, Number in family, Expiration date)

    Plan # is the key of the relation. Most keys in this data model are some type of number. The keys are always underlined. Pay special attention to the keys of the weak entity and the subtype entities.

    (b) Evaluate each relation for normalization criteria. Does the relation have more than one theme? When updated, will this relation have modification anomalies?

2. Now you will show each relationship with the relational model. You'll start with the 1:1 relationship of FAMILY PLAN to CUSTOMER. Lynn wants to use the Plan # to get the Cust #. Modify the FAMILY PLAN relation to show this relationship.

3. Which modifications do you need to make to CUSTOMER and PASSES to show the relationship between them? Rewrite the modified relation.

4. How is the relationship between CUSTOMER and CONTACTS similar to and different from the relationship between CUSTOMER and PASSES?

5. Next, you'll represent the relationships between CUSTOMER and EQUIPMENT, and CUSTOMER and CLASS.
    (a) What will you need to do differently than for a 1:1 or 1:N relationship?
    (b) Show the new relations.

6. Lynn wants to send a coupon for a free equipment rental to customers who refer other customers. How will you modify the CUSTOMER relation to show this relationship?

7. The last type of relationship you need to represent in the relational model is the IS-A relationship.
    (a) Do your relations in Question #1 correctly represent the generalization hierarchies of CONTACTS and CLASS? Verify your answer.
    (b) If you need to modify the relations, rewrite them.

8. You now have all of the relations in relational model form. The next step is to draw a data structure design. This will be very straightforward. The entities from the data model will be relations in the data structure design. The symbols designating subtypes and mandatory and optional requirements in the data model will be the same in the data structure design.

(a) Since all relations are connected to CUSTOMER, start by putting the CUSTOMER relation in the middle of a clean sheet of paper. There is no specified place for relations in a data structure design. The following questions will help organize your design.

(b) To the upper-left side of CUSTOMER, put PASSES. Show the type of relationship and whether it's mandatory or optional. Your diagram should look similar to Figure 2.

PROFESSOR

| Prof-name | Phone | Dept |

STUDENT

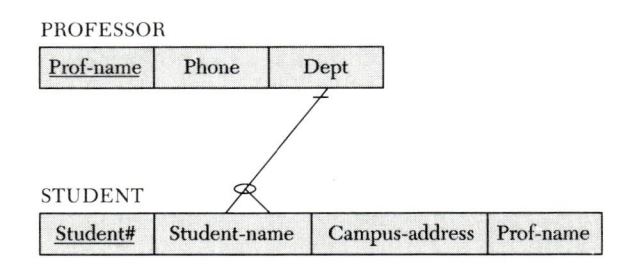

| Student# | Student-name | Campus-address | Prof-name |

FIGURE 2
Example of data structure diagram

9. Put the relation FAMILY PLAN directly above CUSTOMER. Show its 1:1 relation to CUSTOMER and designate its mandatory and optional requirements.

10. Put the relation of EQUIPMENT and the intersection relation to the upper-right side of CUSTOMER. An example of this part of the design is shown in Figure 3.

STUDENT

| SID | . . . |

CLASS

| Class# | . . . |

STU-CLASS
(Intersection relation)

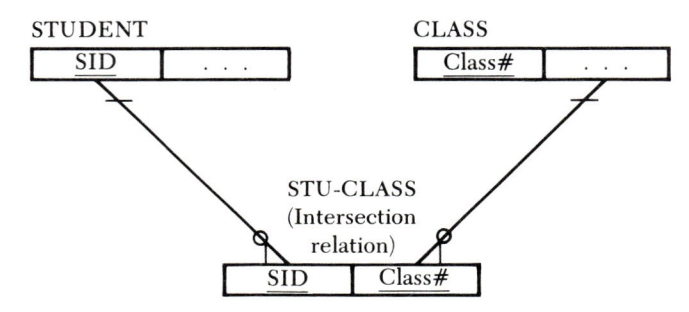

| SID | Class# |

FIGURE 3
Data structure diagram for STUDENT/CLASS relationship

11. (a) To the lower-left side of CUSTOMER, show the relationship between CUSTOMER and CLASS.
    (b) Show the relationship between CLASS and its subtypes.

12. Finish your data structure design by adding the generalization relation of CONTACTS to the lower-right side of CUSTOMER.

The final phase of the development process is implementation. The primary task of implementation is to construct the system according to the design. Hardware is installed, programs are developed, procedures are documented, and personnel are hired and trained.

CASE 5
TRANSFORMING A SEMANTIC OBJECT DATA MODEL INTO A RELATIONAL DATABASE DESIGN

In this case you will be given a semantic object data model for a direct-mail system to be used at Northern Star Expeditions. The data model is a representation of the user's view of the data. The database design is a representation of the computer's view of the data. The database design is expressed as a DBMS-independent description of the data that is to be stored in the database, the relationships among the data, and the data constraints. Keeping the description independent of particular DBMS structures ensures that the design is determined only by user requirements and not by peculiarities or limitations of the DBMS to be used.

You will use another model, the relational model, to develop a DBMS-independent database design. In order to successfully transform the semantic object data model into a relational database design, you will need to know the normalization criteria covered in Chapter 6 of the text and the techniques for transforming data models into DBMS-independent designs covered in Chapter 7.

Specifically, in this part of the case study you will:
- Transform each type of semantic object into a data structure design using the relational data model
- Establish a relation or set of relations for each semantic object
- Evaluate the relations for normalization criteria
- Complete a data structure design

Lynn Lander decided he wanted to start a small direct-mail program, so he discussed his idea with the information systems consultant. They decided it would be a great opportunity to build a small database-processing system. If it met Lynn's needs, then it could be expanded to include other business functions.

The direct-mail program would include three parts. One part would be the mailings that are identified by piece number. There would be three kinds of mailings: one each for course and equipment information and one that would combine course and equipment information. The combined mailing would usually be sent to potential new customers. The second part would be a new order form. By using this form, Lynn could keep track of what each customer ordered (equipment and courses) and related shipping costs. The third part of the program would be to hire a part-time sales representative. This person would take orders and process them. The office manager would do some of these duties when the sales representative was not working.

Figure 1 shows the data model for the direct-mail program. Look carefully at the objects and properties to see the relationships between the different parts of the direct-mail program.

Questions
1. Which type of object is each of the objects in Figure 1?

2. You'll start transforming the data model into a relational database design with the object ITEM. The questions will guide you in transforming each type of object. Then you will combine all the relations into a data structure design. The transformation process is algorithmic. That means there are specific rules to follow in a specific order. Once you know what type an object is, you can apply the rules to transform it into a relation. You should review the rules from the text for each type of object as you transform it. Starting with the

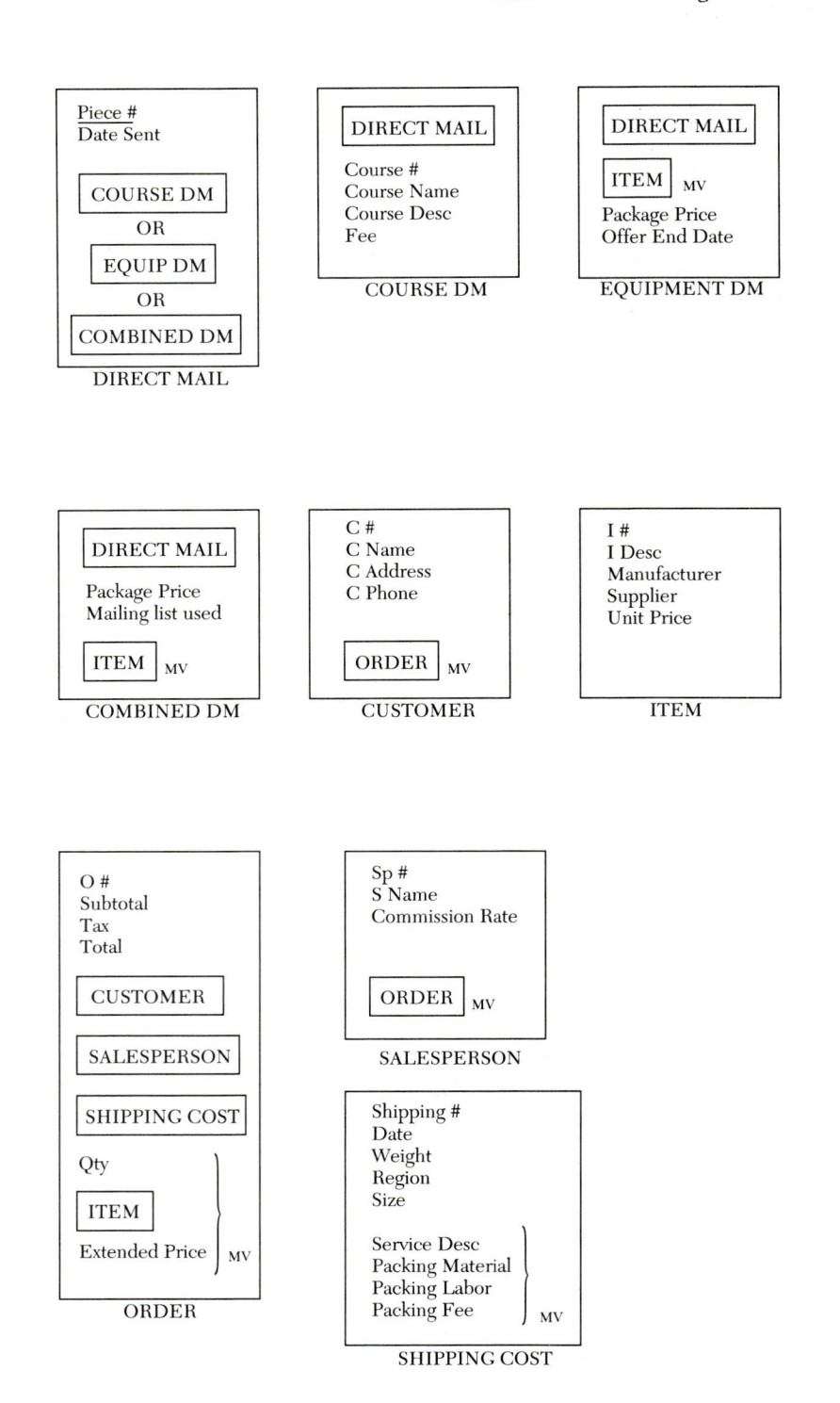

Case 5 - Transforming a Semantic Object Data Model

DIRECT MAIL
- Piece #
- Date Sent
- [COURSE DM] OR [EQUIP DM] OR [COMBINED DM]

COURSE DM
- DIRECT MAIL
- Course #
- Course Name
- Course Desc
- Fee

EQUIPMENT DM
- DIRECT MAIL
- ITEM | MV
- Package Price
- Offer End Date

COMBINED DM
- DIRECT MAIL
- Package Price
- Mailing list used
- ITEM | MV

CUSTOMER
- C #
- C Name
- C Address
- C Phone
- ORDER | MV

ITEM
- I #
- I Desc
- Manufacturer
- Supplier
- Unit Price

ORDER
- O #
- Subtotal
- Tax
- Total
- CUSTOMER
- SALESPERSON
- SHIPPING COST
- { Qty, ITEM, Extended Price } MV

SALESPERSON
- Sp #
- S Name
- Commission Rate
- ORDER | MV

SHIPPING COST
- Shipping #
- Date
- Weight
- Region
- Size
- { Service Desc, Packing Material, Packing Labor, Packing Fee } MV

FIGURE 1

Case 5 - Transforming a Semantic Object Data Model   41

simple object ITEM, two things to remember are that the object name becomes the relation name and the properties become the attributes of the table. Since each property of ITEM is single-valued, the properties fit into the cells of the relation.

Figure 2 is an example of a simple object, BUS PASS:

BUS PASS

Pass #	Month	Route	Fee

FIGURE 2

   (a) Diagram ITEM like the example BUS PASS.

3. The next object to transform is the composite object of SHIPPING COST.
   (a) How many relations will you need to transform this object?
   (b) Why do you need this many?
   (c) What is the key for the composite group?
   (d) Diagram the relations.

4. Next, you will transform into relations the special case of the compound objects: association objects.
   (a) Pattern the association object transformation after the general transformation in Figure 3. Include only the relations pertaining to the association part of the objects.

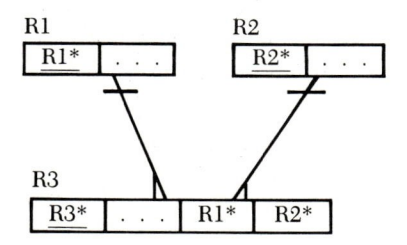

R1
| R1* | . . . |

R2
| R2* | . . . |

R3
| R3* | . . . | R1* | R2* |

FIGURE 3
General transformation of association object into relations

5. The next step is to transform the generalization hierarchy of DIRECT MAIL. Figure 4 shows an example of a generalization hierarchy of an object: STUDENT CLUB:

STUDENT CLUB

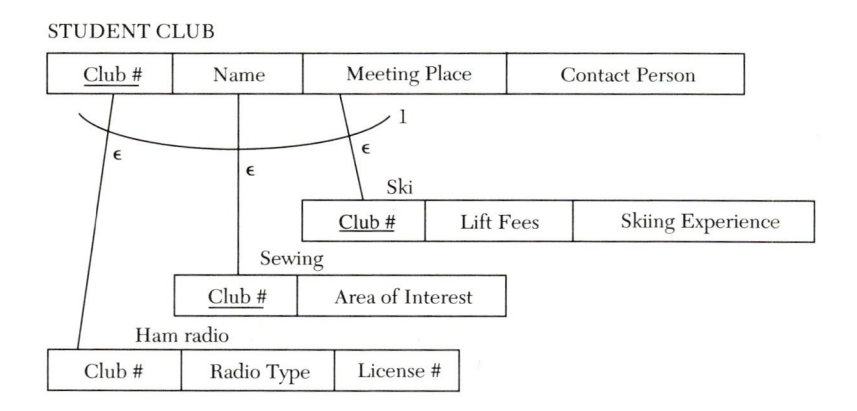

| Club # | Name | Meeting Place | Contact Person |

Ski

| Club # | Lift Fees | Skiing Experience |

Sewing

| Club # | Area of Interest |

Ham radio

| Club # | Radio Type | License # |

FIGURE 4

The curved line designates the subtypes and the 1 means the clubs are mutually exclusive.
  (a) Diagram the DIRECT MAIL generalization hierarchy without including the ITEM object.

6. Look at the association relation you developed in Question #4.
   (a) Is the SALESPERSON relation complete in its transformation?
   (b) Is the CUSTOMER relation complete in its transformation?
   (c) ORDER is a hybrid object. How many relations are in its transformation? Diagram the composite group.

7. You have transformed each of the objects into a relation. Check that each relation is in DK/NF form. Explain how the relations meet this criteria or explain the changes you made.

8. The next step is creating a data structure diagram. Since most of the objects are connected to ORDER, put the ORDER relation at the top of the page. When you complete the data structure design for the ORDER relation, most of the data structure diagram will be done.

9. Connect the ITEM relation to DIRECT MAIL. Pay attention to the foreign keys when you connect COMBINED DM and EQUIPMENT DM to ITEM. This will complete your data structure diagram.

With a complete design you are now ready for the implementation stage. The final phase of the development process is implementation. The primary task of implementation is to construct the system according to the design. Hardware is installed, programs are developed, procedures are documented, and personnel are hired and trained.

CASE 6
PARTIAL IMPLEMENTATION OF A RELATIONAL DATABASE DESIGN

You have learned the essential skill of creating a DBMS-independent data structure design. Now you must learn the rules of the DBMS so you can implement the database for the user.

In cases 4 and 5 you created DBMS-independent data structure designs using the relational model. The next step is to implement the database using a DBMS. This case uses the DBMS of Paradox. If you are using a different DBMS, you can still complete this case. You will follow the sequence of implementation steps, but disregard the instructions specific to the Paradox software.

Even though Paradox is designed for the relational data model, you will need to modify the data structure diagrams you developed in order to use them with Paradox. The relational model cannot be implemented exactly as it is because of the rules of the Paradox software. Most of the changes are needed to improve the speed of processing.

Specifically, in this case you will:
- Create tables
- Create a standard form
- Create a standard report
- See how the parts of a partial implementation work together

Lynn Lander wants to track customers who have family passes. He wants an easy way to enter the data and a printed list of the customers who have family passes for the ski instructors. You will create a data entry form that has customer and family information on it and a simple report listing the customers' names and addresses.

You will use the FAMILY PLAN and CUSTOMER relations in the Case 4 data structure design for this partial implementation plan. The following questions will lead you through the process. Even though the commands needed to complete the exercises are provided, you should be familiar with Paradox before starting this case.

Questions for the Partial Implementation Plan
1. The first step is to define the tables. The first table you will create is C6-fam (for the FAMILY PLAN relation).

    These are the attributes in the FAMILY PLAN relation from Case 4:
    Plan#, # in Family, Expiration Date, and *Cust#*.

    Move the attribute Cust# to the beginning of the relation. Because Cust# is a foreign key, it has to be a keyed field in the C6-fam table. When you move Cust#, you change the data structure design to a DBMS-dependent design. Paradox requires that all keyed fields are the first fields in the tables.

    > *Create the C6-fam table with the fields* Cust#, Plan#, # in Family, and Expiration Date. Use appropriate field types and key the Cust# and Plan# fields.

2. Next, you will create the C6-cust table. The attributes in the CUSTOMER relation from Case 4 are *Cust#*, Name, Address, and Referred-by. In the C6-cust table, the key, *Cust#*, remains the same. The attributes of Name and Address must be split into separate parts and each part given a field name. The separate fields allow Paradox to manipulate the data independently. For the Name attribute, use the field names Fname and Lname. For the Address attribute, use the fields Address, City, State, and Zip. Don't include the Referred-by field. Use data definitions you think are reasonable. Remember to put an asterisk beside the key field.

> Create table C6-cust. Cust# is the key field. The other fields are Fname, Lname, Address, City, State, and Zip. Use appropriate field types.

3. Now that you have the tables set up, the next step is to enter data into them. Paradox's default data entry method is to enter the data directly into the tables. This is not easy for users because the tables do not look like forms. You will use Paradox's standard form to enter data.

If you had a copy of a form the user wanted to continue using, you could create a standard form similar to it on the screen. Since you don't have a form, you need to think about the entities in the user's environment. When Lynn thinks of a family pass program, he probably thinks of the object CUSTOMER first, then about the object FAMILY PASS. Using this logic, the customer information should appear first on the form, followed by the family pass information. To create a standard form with the CUSTOMER information first and the FAMILY PASS information second, you can create a source table. The user enters data into the source table, so it is the source of the user's information. The source table has target tables, which in this case are C6-cust and C6-fam. Associated with every source table is a map table. The map table tells the source table where to put the information in the target tables. It isn't as complicated as it sounds. The first step is to construct the source table as if you were constructing an answer table. You need to create a query in the workspace that represents the source table.

> F10|Ask|C6-cust, check all the fields and put an example element in the Cust# field.
> F10|Ask|C6-fam, put same example element in the Cust# field and check the rest of the fields. Do **not** press F2.

4. The next step is to create the source table and the map. With the query tables on the screen, you will create the source table.

Check the map table to see if the fields in the source table are correctly filling the target tables. Use the right arrow key to see the last field of the map table. The Source Field is a list of the fields in C6-cust and C6-fam. The Target Field is the same as the Source Field. The Target Table field should show that each field is filling the table it belongs to. Cust# should be shown filling the C6-cust and the C6-fam tables.

Case 6 - Partial Implementation of a Relational Database Design   45

> **F10**, and select **Modify|MultiEntry|SetUp**. Pick a name for your source table and press **Enter**.
> The top line changes to "Map name:". Pick a name for your map table and press **Enter**.

5. You will use Paradox's standard form to enter data into the source table you created. These are the commands to bring up the standard form:

> **F10|Modify|MultiEntry|Entry|Type in source table name|Enter|**
> Type in map table name|Enter
> The entry table will appear on the screen. To bring up the form, press **F7**.

6. The purpose of the standard form is to make it easy for the user to input data. Use your form to input at least five records. Remember that the Cust# and Plan# are keyed fields, so the entries must be unique. Use the Enter key and the up and down arrow keys to move between fields in the form. Use the backspace key to correct typing errors. When you are finished entering the records, press **F2**.

7. Lynn wants to give a list of the names and addresses of the customers who have a family pass to the ski instructors. You will use Paradox's standard report function to create this report. The standard report lists the information in tabular form with the field names as headings. These are the commands to produce the standard report:

> **F10|Report|Enter (Output)|Type C6-cust|Enter|Enter (Standard report)|Enter (Printer)**

As you can see, the process of implementation is very involved for even a simple data entry form and standard report. That's why the field of database design and processing is so fascinating—it involves fitting all the pieces together so that the whole system works.

PART II

SKAGIT VALLEY AIRPLANE DEALERSHIPS
CASE STUDIES

This section of the casebook has been designed to follow a second business through both the entity relationship and semantic object development processes. Case 7 is an introduction to database processing similar to Case 1. Cases 8 through 12 are about the Skagit Valley Airplane Dealership business. A member of this family-owned business wants to franchise the dealerships. The cases are presented so that you can work through the entire process with this business situation just as you did with Northern Star Expeditions. The question format is the same as in the last 6 cases. This approach allows you to spend more time developing your skills and less time trying to understand the instructions than you did in the first set of cases.

Again, you will see Paradox software directions that give examples of database processing implementation. All of the instructions for the Paradox procedures are included in the text. In case 12 you will create tables, a standard form, and a standard report.

BACKGROUND INFORMATION FOR CASES 8, 9, 10, 11, AND 12

"Look, it's a great idea and something we should have been doing long ago. You know it is."

"Sarah, I don't think so. I just don't think this is the right time. We need to conserve our cash."

"Yeah, right. Like the cash we're conserving with Dan's latest adventure in the Alps? How much will we lose on this one? And how bad was the loss last time? $250,000? My big brother, the movie maker."

"Really! Stop it. We got plenty of promotional attention from that movie—the educational stations carried it all over the states."

"That's debatable, Dad, but, OK, suppose I grant you that point. Yeah, take that point. How many dealerships do we have in the United States? Three. All in the Northwest. So, what good is national coverage? Take an example—Los Angeles. Let's suppose that movie actually did air in L.A. like Dan said. How many planes did we sell in L.A. last year? Do you know?"

"No, Sarah, do you?"

"Yeah, I happen to, because I've been looking at the data. In 1990 we sold, in L.A.—are you ready? Five! Five whole airplanes in Los Angeles, a city of seven million people!"

"But, Sarah, in the future . . ."

"Look, Dad, you had a good idea. You've got three kids. Me and my two great-businessmen brothers. So you gave each of us a dealership. Fine. The family owns three airplane dealerships. You and Chris run this one—though we both know how much work Chris puts into it—but that's your affair. Dan runs the dealership in Eugene. He might do all right with it, too, if he were ever there. But he's got all these crazy kid notions about flying movies and acrobatics and air shows and so forth ad nauseam."

"Sarah Marie!!"

"Dan's a great pilot, Dad, we both know that. But he lets his business go down the tubes, and it doesn't need to. Eugene's a great market. He could be making a killing down there with our licenses and your money. Does he? No—he spends piles of dough on dubious promotional ventures. That last one lost us a lot more than $250,000, didn't it? Come on, tell me."

". . ."

"All right, Dad, don't. But, do you know where is he now?"

"He left Switzerland last week."

"No, he left Switzerland two weeks ago. He's parked in Florence, 'Checking out locations'—for his next cash drain, I suppose. I know because I talked to him at 5:00 this morning. Know why I was up at 5:00? Not to talk to my dilettante brother, for sure—I was calling dealers on the East coast looking for hardware for that old Cessna I've already sold. The prices on that stuff have gone through the ROOF!"

"All right, all right. Try me again. What do you want to do?"

Skagit Valley Airplane Dealerships Case Study

"Dad, we've got the exclusive North American distributorship on Zeber planes—as you well know since you did the deal. But right now, it's a wasting asset. We're not even starting to tap the potential on that agreement. Sure, we sell planes to other dealers, and we make some money on that—good thing, given my spendthrift brother—but we could be doing so much more.

"Four years ago you set me up in that dealership in Everett. There was nothing going on up there. And, I've built a good business . . ."

"You're right, Sarah, you've done a great job. I know that. It wasn't much of a market, or at least, so I thought, but you've pulled rabbits out of the hat up there and it's a solid business. No question about it."

"OK, here's the thing. It's kind of a formula, but it works. We bring in the customers on the charter business. We sell the classes separately, or as a package deal—the ground class, the supervised flying, and the solos—just to get the people excited about flying, and we lease the planes. We keep the planes busy full time during the season—when we need to, we know who to call to fill our lease roster. That's part one.

"Next, we sell planes to the class graduates—at least some of them. By the end of the school series, we know who's driving the new BMWs and who's driving the '84 Hondas, and we talk to the BMW crowd about the advantages of ownership. We sell them on their ability to lease the planes back through us. So, they buy the planes and we put them into the lease fleet. That's part two. At this point we've sold more planes and added them to our lease fleet, thus increasing our lease capacity and so adding to our customer base. And, unlike Dan's movies, we make money on every part of the deal.

"That brings me to part three. We sell equipment, hanger space, repairs, anything I can get my hands on to vertically integrate the business. I'd buy the airport if I could raise the money—and, by the way, I might—"

"WHAT? Now you want to buy the airport? There's nothing to that airport! They don't even have a decent grocery store. What do they want for it?"

"No, Dad, let's forget about the airport—at least for now.

"Here's what's bothering me: It works. My formula works. But there's only so much room in the Everett Airport. There's only so many planes I can sell and support without flooding that market and ruining the experience for everybody. The flying club is already moaning and groaning about the planes in their hangers. Plus, the weather. At least eight months of the year, it's tough."

"Tell me about it. When you kids were young, we starved in the winter. We did. I just wish your mother had lived to . . ."

"Me, too, Dad, me, too. But she didn't. And life goes on. And besides, with all of that work and sacrificing, don't we have a responsibility to keep it moving? Should we be sitting on this opportunity? Think about it. We have a great formula and the NORTH AMERICAN distributorship for the hottest new line of airplanes in years. Easy to fly and great performers. Put the formula together with this license and we're sitting on a goldmine! Literally."

"OK, OK, you're wearing me down. I'm an old man, but I'm intrigued. You'd think I'd have a little peace of mind and rest in my old age."

"Baloney. You love this business like I do. Now, listen . . . "

Part 2

"Ryan, the key to this business is timing and accuracy—pinpoint accuracy. We've got to be able to make our moves at the last possible moment and then make them count. Like in a race. I want to have the fastest turnaround on our plane inventory of anybody in the business. I want to get our hit rate up on direct mail. I want to make sure that everybody who owns a SR10 NAVIGATOR receives the brochure about the SR10 NAVIGATOR upgrade within two weeks of the announcement, and ONLY those people receive that brochure. I want to cut the holding costs on our parts inventory to half of what they are now. I want to push the suppliers for overnight delivery on the parts we want—not on the parts they choose. I want the dealerships to share inventory data so that we can lower our overall inventory size. This industry has been run like a gentlemen's club for too long.

"Now, as best as I can tell, computers are going to help us. Certainly they helped us in Everett. And that's why I want you to assemble a team and start building these systems."

"Whoa!! Whoa!! You know what the carpenters say?"

"No, what?"

"Measure twice and cut once. Let's take some time and figure out what we need and where we're going."

"Oh, really, Ryan. You didn't mess around like that for me in Everett. Let's get rolling. I need the systems ASAP!"

"Nope. Sorry. No can do. Find another technotwit."

Sarah sighed heavily and looked out the window at the puddles of water in the parking lot. It was a dreary, cold day. "Typical June day in Seattle," she thought. "You know, Ryan, in some places it's sunny and warm on June 17th. Why do we live here?"

"Sarah, how much time do you have now?"

"About an hour."

"OK, take that hour and explain the total concept to me. I need more details about what you want to do."

"Fine. First, nobody's yet approved this plan. Dad said he'd consider it, and he wants to involve Dan and Chris, though I doubt that's wise. Still, he's got control and that's what he wants. So, here's the idea so far."

During the next hour, Sarah explained her plan. As she had told her father, she wanted to apply her formula for running an airplane dealership in conjunction with their exclusive distributorship for Zeber Airplanes. Her idea was to build a network of airplane dealer franchises. Each franchise would receive, as part of the franchise, preferred access and prices for Zeber planes, management training for building and running the dealership, sales training for its salespeople, and national advertising and other marketing exposure (like Dan's movies) on a co-op basis. Each franchise would also receive a group of information systems that would not only facilitate the management of the dealership but would also interconnect the dealerships so that they could share data on customers, sales, suppliers, and inventory and communicate with one another for other purposes.

Sarah wanted to copy the systems she was using in Everett, plus develop a number of others. She wanted each salesperson to have a word processing application for sales activities as well as access to a personal database. Each salesperson could then look up customers by name or number, find out their address and phone, if they've taken classes or charters, the airplanes and flight routes they have flown, and if they own and/or lease a plane. She wanted the employees of each dealership to share a charter reservation system for all of their planes. This system needed to produce reports on plane activity, including an accounting of revenue generated and owed to the plane owners.

Finally, she wanted the franchises to share plane and equipment inventory data. She wanted the dealerships to be able to communicate with one another so that they could lease each other's planes when necessary, so that they could share data regarding sales trends and possible problems, and so that they could share maintenance and repair information. In general, she wanted to build a sense of esprit de corps among the franchisees.

Sarah also wanted to provide each dealership with a common accounting information system. This system would generate files of data that Skagit Valley could process to compute franchise fees (she anticipated charging the franchisees a percentage of their revenue). A common accounting system would make those computations easier to perform and control.

Part 3

"This is Mark Makato of Skagit Valley returning Wayne Zeber's call."

"Yes, Mr. Makato. Just a minute, please. He's on his way up from the factory floor. I'll connect you in a moment."

While Mark waited, he thought about Sarah. "What a daughter!" he mused. "I guess I should turn this company over to her in a few more years. Dan will scream bloody murder; he thinks it's already his. He is the oldest and it could have been his, but she's got the head for business. She'll do fine in a few more years. I just need to keep her from running off half-cocked chasing ideas like this franchise thing. I wonder what Wayne wants? Hmmm."

"Mark, this is Wayne."

"Hi, Wayne, how you doing? We late on our payments or something?"

"Nah, heavens, no. You're fine, as always. I do need to talk with you though."

"Well, you've got me. What's up?"

"Well, you know we're getting great reviews on our planes."

"No doubt about it."

"We've got a couple more models to round out the line and then we're pretty much set, design-wise, for a few years. Everybody's telling me we could be selling a lot more planes."

"Well, I think that's true. But, we're selling all the planes you can make as it is. How many more planes can you turn out?"

"That's just it. We're in the process of deciding to increase our production. We're looking at some options that would triple our production capacity in twenty-four months. With substantial increases before then."

"Hmmm. Those are big jumps; can you handle them?"

"Not sure, just yet. But maybe. Anyway, if we do, how many of those additional planes can you sell? How would you go about it?"

"Wayne, I'd like to think about it. There are ways."

"Well, Mark, you've been good to us. You were one of the first to believe in us and our designs, and because of that, and, frankly, also because of the money you put up front, we gave you that exclusive agreement. You must know I'd never sign that agreement today.

"The point is, and I don't want to jerk you around, but, if we triple our production facility, I've got to know that you can sell the planes. And I don't see how you can do it. So, I'm thinking I need to start developing relationships with other dealers. But, before you get excited, I don't mean your competitors there in the Northwest. That's your territory and it will stay that way. But, at this point in our growth, we need national exposure."

"Wayne, this is an odd coincidence. We've been kicking around an idea that might provide both of us just that exposure. How fast are you moving on this?"

"We want to make a decision by the end of July or early August."

"How about this, Wayne? Let me think this situation through for a week or so and I'll get back to you. I don't think our exclusive relationship needs to be over just yet. Actually, the timing could be perfect. Are you in next week, say Thursday?"

"Let me check . . . Yeah, fine."

"OK, I'll call you then, and if we decide to go ahead with our idea, Sarah and I will come out and brief you on it. By mid-July, latest."

"All right, I'll be here. Let me know."

Mark hung up the phone and rocked back in his chair. He immediately leaned forward, picked the phone up again and buzzed the outer office. "Allisa, would you get Sarah on the phone for me. She's probably in her car driving back to Everett."

While he waited, he mused. "Could that franchise idea make sense? Could we build it fast enough? Could we sell three times the planes? Maybe we should just sell the exclusivity back to Zeber? That pretty much makes us a permanent regional dealer. Is that bad? What does Sarah really want to do? Does she know we'd be betting the farm?"

The phone buzzed. "Mark, I've got Sarah on line two for you."

"Thanks, Allisa."

"Hey, Sarah. Where are you?"

"On my way back to Everett. What's the rush? You never call on my car phone. Did Dan lose another plane?"

"No. I'm thinking about your idea for the franchises. How long will it take for you to pull the whole plan together?"

"I don't know. How about two weeks?"

"No, not soon enough. How about Monday?"

"Next Monday? Good heavens. You taking too much Geritol?"

"Listen, pal, you and I and maybe your brothers need to make some decisions. Wayne Zeber just called me. He is gearing up to make three times as many planes and wants to know if we can sell them." Mark told Sarah the details of his conversation with Wayne Zeber. "So, can you get that plan done by Monday?"

"You betcha."

"I think I'll come up this weekend. I want to fly that new Zeber 500."

"Sorry, Dad. It's chartered. I can give it to you in, maybe, six weeks. Twenty percent discount for family?"

"Uh-huh. What have you got up there I could fly? If you believe the forecast, it's supposed to be sunny and clear."

"Well, how about that Cessna? She'll fly, but she's a little short on hardware."

"Hmm. Think Caroline would like to take her out for the weekend with me?"

"Caroline would love it. She's your granddaughter—she flies better than Dan did at her age."

"Sure. We'll go over to Roche Harbor. Sam will let me land there. Us old folks stick together, you know. You think your plane will fly that far?"

"I'll tell Caroline to be ready Saturday morning. How about seven, since you oldsters get up so early? See you later!" Sarah hung up the phone.

Part 4

"Ryan, this is Sarah. I need to get cracking on that franchise idea I spoke about this afternoon. Dad's on to something, and he wants the outline of a plan by Monday . . . I know it's already Thursday. Can you come up tomorrow and work through the weekend?"

"Is this a proposal or are you paying?" Ryan wasn't about to give up his weekend to develop a bid.

"You can turn your meter on, Ryan. I need help getting this plan together. I thought we'd meet tomorrow and talk it over, then on Saturday, I'll work the general business issues and you work the information systems side. We can combine our work on Sunday afternoon."

CASE 7
INTRODUCTION TO DATABASE PROCESSING

This case study reintroduces you to database processing. The purpose of this case study is twofold: to give you a chance to work through the tutorial for the specific database management system you will be using and to examine sample tables in Paradox.

Specifically, you will:
- Become familiar with the facilities at your school for database processing.
- Work through the tutorial for the specific database management system you will be using.
- If you will be using Paradox, you will retrieve information from the sample tables that are on the floppy disk provided with the casebook. This process is called querying the database.

The time you will need to complete this case can vary greatly. Working through this case could take you as little as fifteen minutes if you already know Paradox. If you worked through Case 1, you should be able to complete it in less than two hours. If you need a Paradox refresher, work through the tutorials provided by Paradox, and then complete the questions about the sample tables on the disk.

Remember, if you are not using Paradox you can go on to Case 8.

For this case study, pretend you are planning a vacation. You've decided to take a chartered adventure trip in either the tropics or the mountains. Now you want specific information about the trips such as the prices and departure dates. The samples tables in this case could be found in a travel agency's database.

We designed for the sample tables without regard to which software package we'd use to implement it. This is called a Database Management System (DBMS) independent design. We then transformed it to a DBMS-dependent design. The word "dependent" means dependent on the software package; in this case, Paradox. It's important to remember that designing a database is a generic process, and implementation is specific to the DBMS.

Questions for Querying Sample Tables
To get started, look at each of the sample tables. By examining the sample tables, you will begin to understand their structure. There are two tables that are used in this case. Each table begins with C7, for Case 7. The first sample table, C7-chart, contains information about the charter number, charter name, price, and departure and return dates. The second sample table, C7-cntry, contains the country and the climate information and the corresponding charter number. You might have noticed that both C7-chart and C7-cntry have a charter number in the tables. This is how the tables are related to each other. You will see why these relationships between the tables are important as you work through the following questions.

To complete the following questions, you will examine the sample tables and then do three queries on the tables. Querying is an excellent way to begin to understand a database design. This means you give the DBMS specific directions to retrieve and present the information you want. At the travel agency you would query the chartered trips database. Querying a database is fun because of the possibilities and also frustrating because of the limitations of the DBMS. Refer to the list of frequently used Paradox commands in Case 1 of this text if you need a refresher.

In questions 5–11 you will examine the structure of the sample tables and the data in the sample tables, do two single-table queries and one linked-table query. In question 5 you will examine the structure of table C7-chart. In question 6 you will examine the structure of table C7-cntry. For questions 7 and 8 you will examine the data in C7-chart and C7-cntry, respectively. You will do a query by selecting specific fields in the table C7-chart for question 9 and do a query using range operators on table C7-chart in question 10. The last question asks you to do a query on the linked tables of C7-chart and C7-cntry. The answers for this case will be the tables you generate from the queries. They will be named C7-1, C7-2, and C7-3. For each question we give the Paradox commands in bold letters.

5. For this question you will look at the table structure of C7-chart. Before doing this, you need to tell Paradox where the table is. After starting the Paradox program, insert the casebook diskette in drive A.

   These are the commands to tell Paradox that the table is on the diskette in drive A.

   > **Tools|More|Directory|(Delete the existing directory with the backspace key) Type a:|Enter|Right Arrow (OK)|Enter.**

   In the lower-right-hand corner you will see the message "The working directory is now a:\."

   Now you can look at the structure of C7-chart. The structure defines the data requirements for each field. These are the commands to bring up the structure table for C7-chart.

   > **Tools|Info|Structure|Enter|Use arrow keys to select the table C7-chart|Enter.**

   Look at each field data requirement to see if it is an alphanumeric field or numeric field or date field. If it's an alphanumeric field, notice how many characters are allowed. Notice which fields are keyed. They have an asterisk in the field type column. When you are done, use **ALT F8** to clear the workspace.

   > **Alt F8**

6. Now you can look at the structure of C7-cntry.

   > **Tools|Info|Structure|Enter|Use arrow keys to select the table name|Enter.**

   Look at each field data requirement to see if it is an alphanumeric field, numeric field, or date field. If it's an alphanumeric field, notice how many characters are allowed. When you are done, use **ALT F8** to clear the workspace.

Case 7 - Introduction to Database Processing　　　　　　　　　　　　　　　　　　　　57

> **Alt F8**

7. Now that you know the structure of the C7-chart table, you will look at the data in the table.

> **View|Enter|Use arrow keys to select C7-chart|Enter**

The table will appear as the first image on the screen. You saw the Return Date field in the structure table, but you don't see it on the screen. By pressing the right arrow key, you will be able to see the Return Date field. Review the data in each field, so you are familiar with it before you start doing queries.

> **Press Right Arrow key five times to see the other fields.**
> **Press Right Arrow to return to the first column.**

8. Examine the data in table C7-cntry while the C7-chart table is still on the screen.

> **F10|View|Enter|Use arrow keys to select C7-cntry|Enter**

C7-cntry will appear as the second image on the screen. Review the data in each field, so you are familiar with it before you start doing queries.

Clear the screen.

> **Alt F8**

9. A powerful aspect of database processing is the ability to query the database. This is the first query on a single table. For this query you will answer the question, "What are the prices and departure dates for each trip in the C7-chart table?"

Paradox uses a method called query by example. This means you create a query table that looks like an example of the answer table you want. To select fields to appear in the answer table, move to each field and press **F6.** F6 is a toggle key: use it to place and delete checkmarks in the query tables.

These are the commands to build a query on the C7-chart table to answer the question:

> **Ask|Enter|Use arrow keys to move to C7-chart|Enter**
> **Right Arrow|Right Arrow|F6|Right Arrow|F6|Right Arrow|F6**

You have created the query table. The checkmarks represent the fields that will be in the answer table. Now execute the query with the Do-It! key.

> **F2**

Answer tables are only temporary tables. When you create the next answer table, this will be deleted, so you must rename it to save it. Rename it C7-1.

> **F10|Tools|Enter (Rename)|Enter (Table)|Enter|Enter (Selecting Answer)|Type A:C7-1**

The table will reappear with C7-1 in the left-most column.

Clear the screen.

> **Alt F8**

10. For the next query determine the trips you can go on if you have $500 and can leave after June 15, 1993. Display the charter name, the price, and the departure date. The first step is to create a query table for C7-chart like you did in Question 9.

> **Ask|Enter|Use arrow keys to move to C7-chart|Enter**

Now you want to indicate that the Charter Name, Price, and Departure Date will be in the answer table. In the Price and Departure Date fields, you will use range operators. Range operators tell Paradox which types of values you want in each field, i.e., the range of values for that field.

> **Right Arrow|Right Arrow|F6|Right Arrow|F6** Type <=500 next to the checkmark|**Right Arrow|F6** Type >6/15/93 beside the checkmark|**F2**

Since Answer tables are temporary tables, you need to rename the table C7-2.

Case 7 - Introduction to Database Processing

> **F10|Tools|Enter (Rename)|Enter (Table)|Enter|Enter (Selecting Answer)|Type A:C7-2**

Clear the screen for the last query.

> **Alt F8**

11. The last query uses linked tables. Linked tables are necessary when the answer to the question requires information from two or more tables. Querying from linked tables is similar to querying from one table, except that you fill out a query by example for each table, and you use example elements to tell Paradox how the tables are linked. Linking tables is a important part of database design. You will learn about it in the upcoming textbook chapters and cases.

For this query assume you received a discount coupon for one Asia Express trip. You want to know how much their trips cost and which countries they go to.

The answer table for this query consists of the Charter Name and the Price fields in the C7-chart table and the Country Name field in the C7-cntry table. These are the commands for setting up the linked tables:

> **Ask|Enter|Use arrow keys to move to C7-chart|Enter**
> **Right Arrow|F5|Type e (for example element)|Right Arrow|F6 Type Asia Express|Right Arrow|F6**

You have done the query by example for the first table. Now you need to add the second table to the query, link it to the first, and designate which fields you want displayed.

> **F10|Ask|Enter|Use arrow keys to move to C7-cntry|Enter**
> **Right Arrow|F6|Right Arrow|Right Arrow|F5|Type e|F2**

Rename the Answer table C7-3.

> **F10|Tools|Enter (Rename)|Enter (Table)|Enter|Enter (Selecting Answer)|Type A:C7-3.**

You should now feel very comfortable with Paradox. As you work through Cases 8, 9, 10, and 11, you will practice database design. In Case 12 you will again use Paradox to implement a part of your design.

CASE 8
ENTITY RELATIONSHIP MODELING

Learning Objectives
The purpose of this case is to investigate the ways in which data modeling contributes to an organization's value. In this case, data modeling will be used as a major component contributing to the value of a franchise business. You will interpret the users' requirements for a database processing system and build the users' data model. This will fulfill the requirements phase of the database development tasks. Specifically, in this case you will:
- Develop a data model that represents part of the data model Sarah has of her business and the franchise plan she wants to create.
- Identify the entities in the data model.
- Identify the properties of the entities.
- Represent the relationships between the entities.
- Create a diagram for the data model.

Questions for Developing the Entity-Relationship Model
The questions for this case are split into two parts. In Part 1 you will create different types of entities and appropriate property lists from the Skagit Valley Airplane Dealership case study. In Part 2 you will create an E-R data model.

While you are answering these questions, remember that Sarah has a mental picture of a data structure for her business. You will be modeling her data model. In other words, she knows what will be important to her in her work environment and the relationships between these things. It's your job to represent what's important to her in entities and properties and then represent the relationships in an E-R diagram. Try to adopt Sarah's vantage point as you answer the following:

Part 1
1. The first step in developing an E-R model is to identify the entity classes, which are collections of entities of the same type. Entity classes will be referred to as entities from here on. Entities are usually represented by nouns in the case study. They are written in all capital letters.
   (a) Reread the case study and identify at least ten possible entities that Sarah will need to track to run a franchise business. Remember that data modeling is as much an art as it is a science. The ten entities you choose might not be the same ones your classmates choose.

2. Each entity has properties, or, as they are sometimes called, attributes, that describe entity characteristics. An identifier is a property that uniquely identifies an object. An example is the social security number for an employee. Many people have the same name, but each person has a unique social security number.
   (a) Choose three of your entities and create a property list for them. Put the identifier as the first property and underline it. Some of the properties you will find in the case study, but others you will have to infer. For instance, Sarah does not mention how she will uniquely identify franchises, so you could infer an identifier such as franchise number.

3. Create instances for two of the entities in Question #2.

4. Relationships are the way entities are associated with one another. The number of entities in the relationship is the degree of the relationship.
   (a) Name the three fundamental types of binary relationships.

Case 8 - Entity Relationship Modeling

    (b) Using the entities OWNER, LEASE, and AIRPLANE, develop the three fundamental types of binary relationships.
    (c) Are your examples HAS-A or IS-A relationships?

5. (a) The E-R Model defines a special type of entity called a weak entity. What is the definition of a weak entity?
    (b) What is a subclass of weak entities?
    (c) Look at your list of entities in Question #1. Are any of them weak entities? If so, name the entity it is dependent on and the type of weak entity it is.
    (d) If none of your entities are weak entities, create a plausible example of both types of weak entities.

6. (a) What are generalization hierarchies?
    (b) Each franchise offers classes. Explain how CLASS fits the generalization hierarchies structure.
    (c) What are these relationships sometimes called?

7. (a) Sarah wants to give a free rental coupon to customers who refer other customers to her business. In order to do this, she must keep track of these customers in the database. Name and define this type of relationship.
    (b) Pick an entity from your answers in Question #1 and describe a situation that would represent this type of relationship.

You have now developed the different types of entities and relationships. You have created property lists and instances. The next step is to represent Sarah's data model of her business in an E-R diagram.

Part 2

There are specific conventions for drawing an E-R diagram. Use Figure 1 as a guide for answering the following:

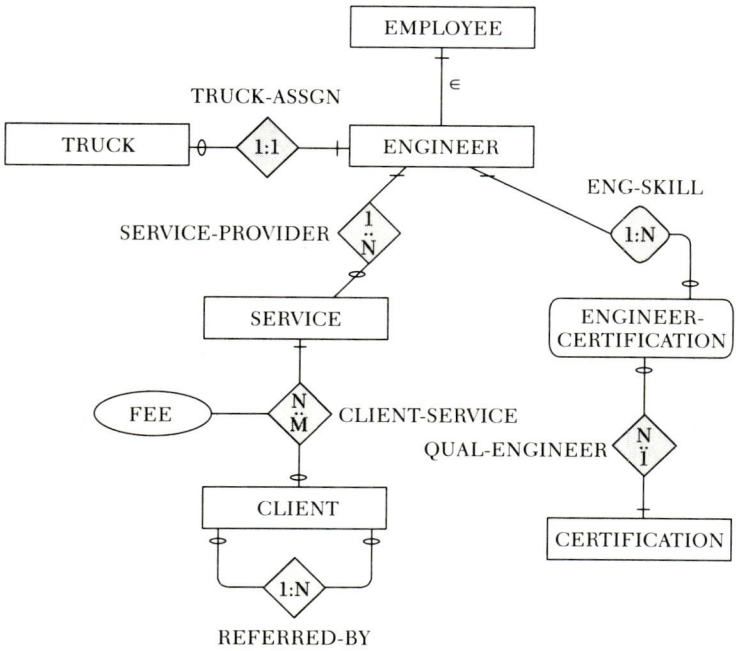

FIGURE 1
Example of entity-relationship diagram

8. Consider the entity of the Skagit Valley Dealership, which would be the HEADQUARTER entity of the franchise business. The headquarters is the connecting link between the Zeber Distributorship and the franchises. Starting at the top of a page, diagram the relationship between these two entities: HEADQUARTER and DISTRIBUTORSHIP. Show the minimum and the maximum cardinality involved and name the relationship.

9. Next consider the FRANCHISE entity. How will the FRANCHISE entity relate to the HEADQUARTERS and DISTRIBUTORSHIP entities? Add FRANCHISE to your diagram, showing the minimum and maximum number of entities involved and name the relationship.

10. It is very important for Headquarters to keep track of the franchise owners' current addresses and phone numbers. There would be no reason to store this information if they didn't own a franchise. This creates a special type of relationship between FRANCHISE and OWNERS. Add OWNERS to your diagram, showing its special relationship to FRANCHISE.

11. Sarah mentioned that she has three different types of classes. Add the relationship of CLASS to FRANCHISE and the three types of classes to your diagram. Show on your diagram whether the classes are required and if they are mutually exclusive.

12. The services the franchise offers ultimately connect the customer to the exclusive distributorship of the Zeber planes.

    Each service the franchise offers will be an entity (CLASS is one example). Decide on the rest of the entities and add them to your diagram. Show the minimum and maximum entities involved in the relationships. Naming the relationships can get redundant at this point and add little meaning to the diagram. This can be omitted.

13. There is a last entity to add to your diagram. It is the very important entity of CUSTOMER. Add CUSTOMER to your diagram, showing the minimum and maximum entities involved. Again, naming the relationships would add little to the diagram.

14. Once a data model has been developed, the designer should consider the possibility of processing restrictions against entities. Give an example of a processing restriction for the updates of (a) a change, (b) an addition, and (c) a deletion. Write up the restrictions as if you were adding documentation to the data model. Include the entity, the processing restriction, and the correct procedure.

15. A completed data model should be evaluated for robustness against the user's data requirements. The questions to use as guides are: "Does this model accurately reflect the user's perceptions and mental models of his activity? Will it help the user respond consistently and successfully to one another and to their clients?" Develop a list of three queries that could be answered from the data model. Explain how the queries can be answered from the data model.

CASE 9
SEMANTIC OBJECT MODELING

Learning Objectives

The purpose of this case study is to interpret a user's requirements for a database processing system and to build the user's data model. In this case Sarah Makato has a series of reports on class offerings at the franchises. She wants the database processing system to produce these reports. Specifically, in this case you will:

- Develop a data model that accurately represents the data model Sarah has of her business.
- Identify the objects in the data model.
- Identify the properties of the objects.
- Represent the relationships between the objects.
- Create a diagram for the data model.

The major goal of database development during the requirements phase is to build a data model that documents the things that are to be represented in the database, to determine the characteristics of those things that need to be stored, and to determine the relationships among them. The following questions will guide you in developing a semantic object data model.

A semantic object is one that models, in part, the meaning of the users' data. A semantic object (referred to as object) is a named collection of properties that sufficiently describes a distinct identity. Objects are shown in portrait-oriented rectangles. The name of the object appears above or beneath the rectangle. Properties are written inside the rectangle. These diagrams are used by development teams to summarize the structure of objects and to present those structures visually.

We'll use a bottom-up approach to develop this data model. We'll examine the application interface: the reports needed to track the franchise businesses. Then we'll work backwards, or reverse engineer, to derive the object structure. This approach is based on the theory that if you know how the users view their interface to the system, you can figure out what must be stored in the database.

The purpose of this case study is twofold. In Part 1 you will develop a set of objects from a set of reports, and in Part 2 you will have the opportunity to develop the remaining types of objects from a report. This will not be a comprehensive data model of the Skagit Valley Airplane Dealership. When you finish, you will know how to develop a complete data model and can do that at a later date.

Part 1

Ryan has created a series of prototype reports for the franchise business. He has presented these reports to Sarah and, after minor modifications, obtained her approval. Consider this report:

```
                    HEADQUARTERS
                 SKAGIT VALLEY AIRPLANES

                  Sarah Makato, President

100 Flight Ave        767-7766

FRANCHISE             OWNER                PHONE

Bayside Airplanes     Ted Myers            243-3112
Pepper's Planes       Jack Pepper          784-4532
A-OK Airplanes        Sandra Phillips      344-3443
```

1. (a) What object does this report seem to be about? The title is usually a good indicator of an underlying object.

   (b) What is Sarah tracking with this report? Remember, an object is the representation of an important entity in the users' work environment—if Sarah wants a report on franchises, then franchise is an object. What is the relationship between the two objects?

   (c) Diagram both objects. Each object has properties shown on the form, but this is only the first form. Following forms may show more properties for these objects. For your first draft of the object diagrams, it's convenient to put the name of the object at the top and draw a rectangle without a bottom line. This way you can list the properties as you find them. For your final diagram you will recopy the diagrams putting the non-object properties first, the object properties below them, and the composite groups last. The object name is placed below the rectangle.

Example of developing diagrams:

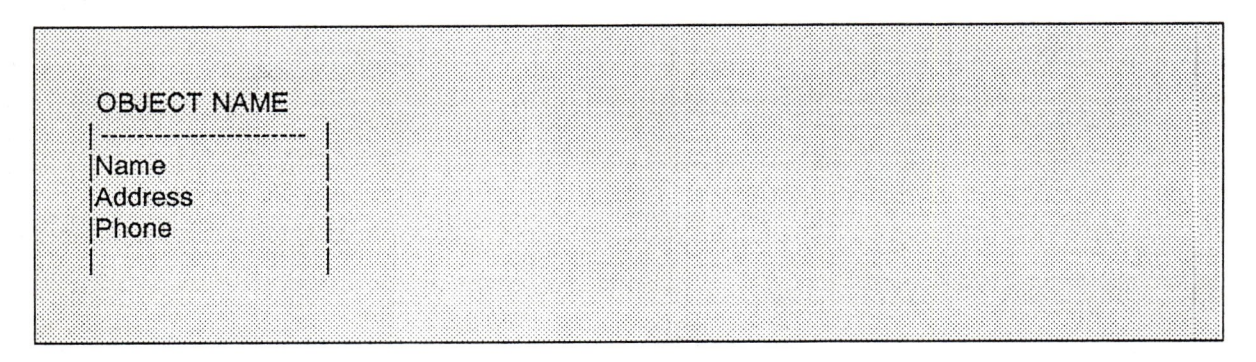

```
OBJECT NAME
|--------------------|
|Name                |
|Address             |
|Phone               |
|                    |
```

2. For thirty days after a customer has taken a class at any franchise, they get a discount of 20% on the purchase of Zeber planes. The franchises send their current class lists of customers to Headquarters. Headquarters sends out the brochures and discount coupons.

Case 9 - Semantic Object Modeling 65

This is the form that is used:

```
FRANCHISE MONTHLY CLASS LIST OF CUSTOMERS

Bayside Airplanes 1001 Bluebay Drive
Ted Myers, Owner 243-3112

CUST#        CUSTOMER          ADDRESS            PHONE
10134        Duke, Michael     2 Kaliper Lane     856-3421
10167        Jasper, Patty     89 Sunset Drive    855-5588
10172        Xing, Debbie      52 Bloomer Street  855-7889
```

- (a) What is the relationship between a franchise and its customers?
- (b) Update the FRANCHISE object.
- (c) Create a new object: CUSTOMER. Will this new object have FRANCHISE in it? How can you tell from the form?

3. Each franchise maintains a current list of class schedules. They keep the list posted in the franchise office and send one to Headquarters. The form looks like this:

```
FRANCHISE CLASS SCHEDULES

Bayside Airplanes 1001 Bluebay Drive
Ted Myers, Owner 243-3112

CLASS        CLASS #    DAY    TIMES           BEG DATE    FEE

Ground       691123     MW     6:00-9:00PM     6/6/91      $350
Supervised   791234     TTH    1:00-5:00PM     7/10/91     $500
Solo         891345     SAT    9:00AM-5:00PM   8/15/91     $250
```

- (a) How is this form similar to the form in question #2?
- (b) Update FRANCHISE and create a new object as you did in #2.

4. One of the services Skagit Valley Airplane Dealerships offer their customers is a full range of certification classes. Not all of the franchises offer each class, so Headquarters provides a matching service. Since most customers are avid amateur pilots, they don't mind traveling for a specific class. If a customer requests a class the franchise doesn't offer, the franchise sends the request to Headquarters. When Headquarters makes a match, it sends the customer this form letter:

> Xing, Debbie
> 52 Bloomer Street
> Flight City, WA 98032
>
> Dear Debbie,
>
> The Class I Acrobatic and Small Engine Maintenance certification classes that you requested are being offered by Pepper's Planes and A-OK Airplanes, respectively. The class registration slips are enclosed. The times, dates, and class requirements are listed separately for your convenience.
>
> The Skagit Valley Airplane Dealerships offer every certification class needed in the state of Washington. We hope you enjoy your class and obtain your desired certification.
>
> Happy flying!
>
> Sarah Makato
> President
>
> SM/ghi
>
> Enclosure

(a) How many classes and franchises can one customer be associated with?
(b) Update your CUSTOMER object.
(c) What is the relationship between CLASS and CUSTOMER? Do any of the forms explicitly show the relationship? There are no one-way relationships. If CUSTOMER has a relationship with CLASS, then the reverse is true. Sometimes a relationship that exists is not needed by the user, so it doesn't belong in the data model. In this case it's very obvious that a class would have many customers.
(d) Update your CLASS object.

5. The final form in the set is shown below. This form lists customers' names sorted in alphabetical order with their addresses and phone numbers.

> Bayside Planes
> Directory # 592
> June 1, 1991
>
> | CUSTOMER | ADDRESS | PHONE |
> |---|---|---|
> | Agis, Natalie | 34 Forest Lane | 565-6655 |
> | Akanamer, Joe | 470 Egin Road | 567-3321 |
> | Attabar, Pete | 3 Miter Road | 565-8937 |

Case 9 - Semantic Object Modeling

67

    (a)   This directory is not a report about a customer. It's a report about a group of customers: a report about the franchise's customer list. What is the underlying object?

    (b)   What are the four properties shown for the object? (Hint: They are not customer, address, and phone.)

    (c)   Diagram this object.

6. You now have all of the objects diagramed for this set of reports. Look over the forms and the objects to check for omissions and/or correct relationships. Redraw your objects as explained in Question #1.

You have successfully developed a small semantic object data model. This completes the major portion of the requirements stage of the database design project.

Part 2

In Part 1 you developed objects that supported the forms. There are other types of objects than the ones that you developed. In Part 2 you will develop each type of object.

7. What type of objects did you develop in Part 1? Why do you think the objects were similar?

8. Another part of the franchise business is charters. Whenever a plane comes in from a charter, it is cleaned. The maintenance person goes to the supply counter and checks out a cleaning package. The package contains a ladder, vacuum, bucket, and cleaning solution bottle. The checkout form looks like this:

```
CLEANING EQUIPMENT

Checkout #:
Name:
Ladder #:
Vacuum #:
Bucket #:
Bottle #:
```

    (a)   What type of object would be represented by this form? What are two characteristics of the properties that support your claim?

    (b)   Diagram the object.

9. Franchises arrange many types of charters. Some are very simple, such as a drop off at a country airport for backpackers or bicyclists. Others are very elaborate. They might include limousine service from the airport, expensive hotels, fine food, and roses. The franchise itemizes the charter bill for the customer. This is the type of bill the customer would receive:

```
                        BAYSIDE AIRPLANES
                         Charter Invoice

Charter Number:      852
Departure Date:      August 15, 1991
Return Date:         August 16, 1991

8/15/91              Airplane                              $ 200.00
                     Pilot                                 $ 300.00
                     Hotel                                 $ 100.00
                     Food
                             Dinner        $ 150.67
                             Room Service  $  45.21
                                                           $ 195.88

8/16/91              Airplane                              $ 200.00
                     Pilot                                 $ 300.00
                     Food
                             Breakfast     $  25.23
                             Lunch         $  40.55
                                                           $  65.78

8/16/91              Subtotal                              $1358.66
                     Tax                                   $ 108.69
                     Total due                             $1467.35
```

  (a) What are the single-valued properties of the CHARTER object?
  (b) What are the multiple-valued properties? Which properties are nested?
  (c) What type of object is CHARTER?
  (d) Diagram the object.

10. The objects in Part 1 were all compound objects. How many subtypes of compound objects are there? Which subtypes are represented in the data model of Part 1?

11. When a customer has a pilot's license and wants to 'rent' a plane for a day, a franchise employee fills out a lease agreement. The customer can also reserve an airplane for an extended time with a lease agreement. A customer may have many lease agreements open at the same time. Each lease is for a specific plane. A plane can be under many leases and usually is. Each lease agreement has a unique number and assigns one customer to one plane.
    (a) What special type of compound object is described above?
    (b) Diagram the objects, using at least three non-object properties. Show the relationship between the customers, the airplanes, and the leases.

12. Many corporations sponsor multiple charters for their employees. The airplanes they use require special on-ground service: repairs, cleaning, and catering. The franchise bills the corporations monthly for the charters and special services. This is a blank form for the monthly invoice:

Case 9 - Semantic Object Modeling

```
                    BAYSIDE AIRPLANES

                  MONTHLY CHARTER INVOICE

Invoice #
Invoice Dates:

Customer Name:
Customer #:
Address:
Phone:

Account Executive:

CHARTER #    DATE    TOTAL PRICE    ON-GROUND    EXTENDED SERVICE    PRICE

Subtotal:
Tax:
Total Due:
```

(a) Some of these properties you have seen before in other objects. That means this object will have object properties. Assume that ACCOUNT EXECUTIVE is an object. Also assume that on-ground service and extended price are not a part of the object CHARTER, but are in the composite group. What type of object is it?

(b) Diagram the object.

(c) Because this object is complicated, you will need to check whether you have shown the relationships correctly. Do this by diagraming the object; then, only looking at the object, create a form with instance properties (names and prices). Check to see if your form is the same as the one above.

(d) Create the CHARTER INVOICE object specification and domain definitions for single-valued properties not in objects. You will need to infer some domains. Follow the standards listed in the textbook in Figure 5–18.

13. Assume the object CLASS is a generalization hierarchy with subtypes of GROUND, SUPERVISED, and SOLO. The classes are mutually exclusive. Diagram CLASS, including differing properties for the subtypes.

You have now developed every type of object that you can use in a data model.

CASE 10
TRANSFORMING AN ENTITY RELATIONSHIP DATA MODEL INTO A RELATIONAL DATABASE DESIGN

In this case you will be given a data model for a customer information database. You will then transform it into a data structure design using the relational model. The data model is a representation of the user's view of the data. The database design is a representation of the computer's view of the data. The database design is expressed as a DBMS-independent description of the data that is to be stored in the database, the relationships among the data, and the data constraints. Keeping the description independent of particular DBMS structures ensures that the design is determined only by user requirements and not by peculiarities or limitations of the DBMS to be used.

You will use another model, the relational model, to develop a DBMS-independent database design. In order to successfully transform the E-R model into a relational database design, you will need to know the normalization criteria covered in Chapter 6 of the text and the techniques for transforming data models into DBMS-independent designs covered in Chapter 7.

Specifically, in this part of the case study you will:
- Establish a relation for each entity
- Designate keys for each relation
- Evaluate relations for normalization criteria
- Express the three types of binary and recursive relationships in terms of relations
- Complete a data structure design

After Mark gave his daughter, Sarah, the go-ahead to develop a plan for franchising the business, the process went quickly. Sarah and Ryan, the information systems consultant, developed a plan for expanding to a franchise business. When they presented the plan to Mark, he was still hesitant about franchising, but could find no fault in their plan. Sarah and Mark then presented the plan to Wayne Zeber, the president of Zeber Airplanes. After the presentation Wayne was willing to retain the exclusive distributorship agreement with them.

Ryan impressed upon Sarah the importance of a well-designed database. He convinced her that they needed to develop and implement a small system to solve the immediate problem. Once they got that system working, they could expand it.

Sarah decided that tracking customer information would be the most beneficial system to develop. The purpose of the system was to identify customers who would potentially purchase Zeber airplanes. She wanted salespeople in each franchise to have access to customer information, such as which classes and charters the customers had taken and their lease agreements. With this information the salespeople could match the customers' interests with a type of Zeber planes.

Ryan and Sarah agreed to start with a bare-bones system. Ryan created a plan to use the minimum amount of information about each entity. He decided to represent FRANCHISE, SALESPERSON, CLASS, CUSTOMER, CHARTER, LEASE, and PLANE SALE entities with an unique number. For the FRANCHISE, OWNER, SALESPERSON, and CUSTOMER entities, he added the properties of name, address, and phone. The information needed for CLASS was date and fee. Each type of class needed different information. GROUND CLASS needed instructor and simulator number; SUPERVISED needed instructor and plane number; and SOLO needed ground crew and plane number. CHARTER was tracked by date and route. LEASE was tracked by

Case 10 - Transforming E-R Models 71

expiration date and rate, and PLANE SALE by date and plane number. Ryan and Sarah knew more information would be needed in the future, but this was enough to develop a useful system.

Sarah also wanted to create incentives for customers to refer potential customers to the franchises. She wanted to offer these customers a substantial discount on an item of their choice at the franchise. In order to do this, she needed to know which customer referred other customers.

Ryan knew he needed a data model and a database design for this small system. The data model he developed is shown in Figure 1.

Questions for Transforming the E-R Data Model Presented in Figure 1 into a Relational Database Design

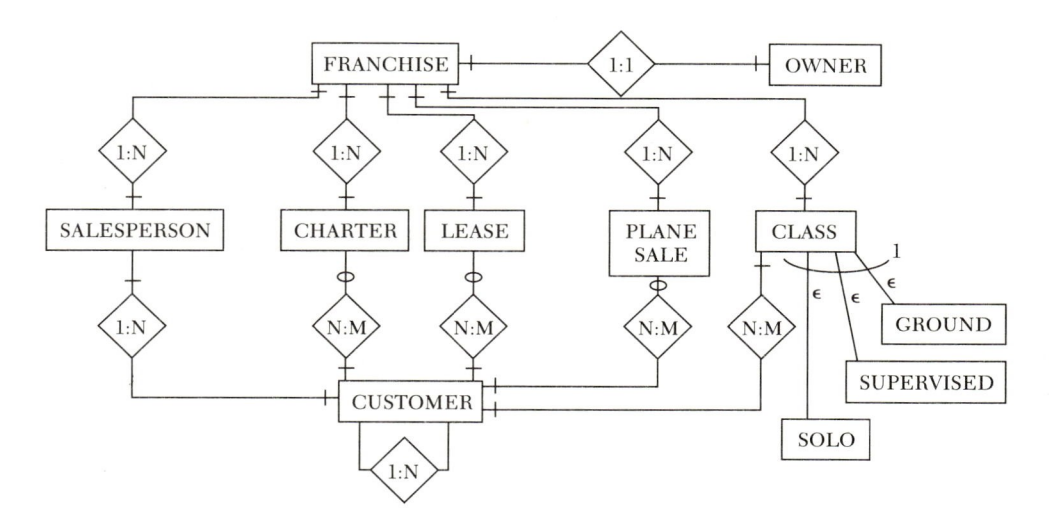

FIGURE 1

1. In general, the representation of entities with the relational model is straightforward. You begin by defining a relation for each entity. The name of the relation is the name of the entity, and the attributes of the relation are the properties of the entity. The property that identifies an entity becomes the key of the relation.

    (a) For each of the entities, create a relation that has a key and its other attributes. Assume the key and attributes are single-valued. An example is the relation SALESPERSON:

    Relation Representing the SALESPERSON Entity

    SALESPERSON (*SP#*, Name, Address, Phone)

    SP # (an abbreviation for SALESPERSON) is the key of the relation. Most keys in this data model are some type of number. The keys are always underlined. Pay special attention to the keys of the weak entity and the subtype entities.

    (b) Evaluate each relation for normalization criteria. Does the relation have more than one theme? When updated, will this relation have modification anomalies?

2. Now you will modify many of the relations to fit into the relational model. You'll start with the 1:N relationships of FRANCHISE to SALESPERSON, CHARTER, LEASE, PLANE SALE, and CLASS.
   (a) How is a relation modified when it is the many side of a 1:N relationship?
   (b) Write out the modified relations for the 1:N relationships with FRANCHISE.

3. Will the OWNER relation needed to be modified? Why or why not?

4. Show the relationship of SALESPERSON to CUSTOMER in the relational model form.

5. The next type of relationship you need to represent in the relational model is the IS-A relationship.
   (a) Do your relations in Question #1 correctly represent the generalization hierarchy of CLASS? Verify your answer.
   (b) If you need to modify the relations, rewrite them.

6. Next, you'll represent the relationships between CUSTOMER and CHARTER, LEASE, PLANE SALE, and CLASS.
   (a) What will you need to do differently than for a 1:1 or 1:N relationship?
   (b) Show the new relations.

7. Sarah wants to encourage customers to refer other customers to the franchises. How will you modify the CUSTOMER relation to show this relationship?

8. You now have all of the relations in relational model form. The next step is to draw a data structure design. This will be very straightforward. The entities from the data model will be relations in the data structure design. The symbols designating subtypes and mandatory and optional requirements in the data model will be the same in the data structure design.
   (a) Start by writing the FRANCHISE relation at the top center of a blank piece of paper. There is no specified place for relations in a data structure design. The following questions will help organize your design. Figure 2 is an example of a data structure design.

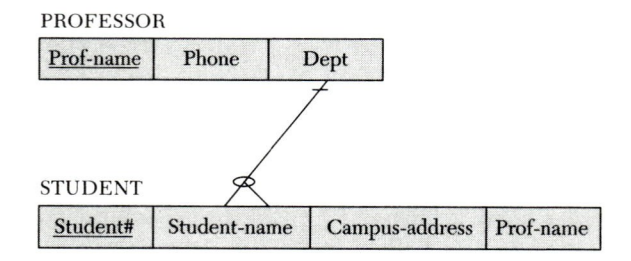

FIGURE 2
Example of data structure diagram

   (b) Connect the OWNER relation to the lower-left side of FRANCHISE.
   (c) Below FRANCHISE put the rest of the relations that are connected to it. Show the type of relationships and whether they are mandatory or optional. Each relationship in your diagram should look similar to Figure 2.

Case 10 - Transforming E-R Models 73

9. Add to your data structure design the generalization relation of CLASS. Designate its mandatory and optional requirements.

10. The next step is to add the intersection relations and the CUSTOMER relation. An example of this part of the design is shown in Figure 3. You may need to put the intersection relation between the two relations it connects.

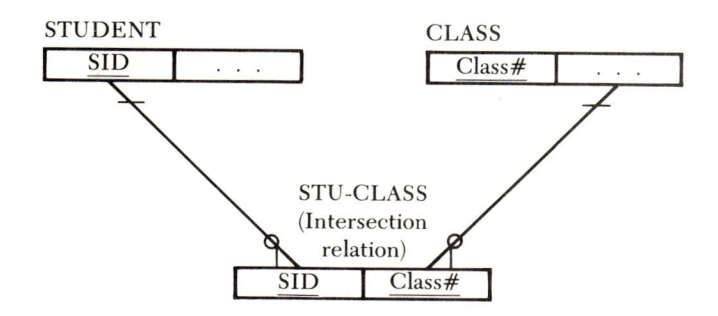

```
       STUDENT                    CLASS
      ┌─────┬─────┐             ┌───────┬─────┐
      │ SID │ ... │             │Class# │ ... │
      └─────┴─────┘             └───────┴─────┘
           \                         /
            \                       /
             \    STU-CLASS        /
              \  (Intersection)   /
               \    relation)    /
                \               /
                 ┌─────┬───────┐
                 │ SID │ Class#│
                 └─────┴───────┘
```

FIGURE 3
Data structure diagram for STUDENT/CLASS relationship

11. The last part of the data structure diagram is the relationship between SALESPERSON and CUSTOMER. Add that now.

The final phase of the development process is implementation. The primary task of implementation is to construct the system according to the design. Hardware is installed, programs are developed, procedures are documented, and personnel are hired and trained.

CASE 11
TRANSFORMING A SEMANTIC OBJECT DATA MODEL INTO A RELATIONAL DATABASE DESIGN

In this case you will be given a data model for a leasing program. The data model is a representation of the user's view of the data. The database design is a representation of the computer's view of the data. The database design is expressed as a DBMS-independent description of the data that is to be stored in the database, the relationships among the data, and the data constraints. Keeping the description independent of particular DBMS structures ensures that the design is determined only by user requirements and not by peculiarities or limitations of the DBMS to be used.

You will use another model, the relational model, to develop a DBMS-independent database design. In order to successfully transform the semantic data model into a relational database design, you will need to know the normalization criteria covered in Chapter 6 of the text and the techniques for transforming data models into DBMS-independent designs covered in Chapter 7.

Specifically, in this part of the case study you will:
- Transform each type of semantic object into a data structure design using the relational data model
- Establish a relation or set of relations for each semantic object
- Evaluate the relations for normalization criteria
- Complete a data structure design

An essential part of Sarah Makato's franchise plan is the leasing program. Through classes and promotions Sarah wants to target individuals and corporations who will buy airplanes and then lease them to the franchise. Both the owners and the franchise will benefit. The owners will have a well-maintained plane and a tax advantage. The franchise will have many planes available to use in its lesson and leasing programs. Sarah set up the lease program with specific criteria. The lease agreement assigns one plane to one customer. It also tracks service fees and charges to the customer or owner. Owners may have multiple leases and own many planes. A customer may have many leases open and airplanes may be under multiple leases. Lease fees are determined by the amount of airtime and a standard route description. These lease fees are paid directly to the owners. The franchise bills its services through the service fees.

Figure 1 shows the data model for the leasing program. Look carefully at the objects and properties to see the relationships between the different parts of the leasing program.

Questions for Transforming the Semantic Object Data Model into a Relational Database Design

1. Which type of object is each of the objects in Figure 1?

2. You'll start transforming the data model into a relational database design with the object ROUTE. The questions will guide you in transforming each type of object. Then you will combine all the relations into a final data structure design. The transformation process is algorithmic. That means there are specific rules to follow in a specific order. Once you know what type an object is, you can apply the rules to transform it into a relation. You should review the rules from the text for each type of object as you transform it. Starting with the simple object ROUTE, two things to remember are that the object name becomes the relation name and the properties become the attributes of the table. Since each property of ROUTE is single-valued, the properties fit into the cells of the relation.

Case 11 - Transforming a Semantic Object Data Model

OWNER
- O - #
- O - Name
- O Address
- O Phone

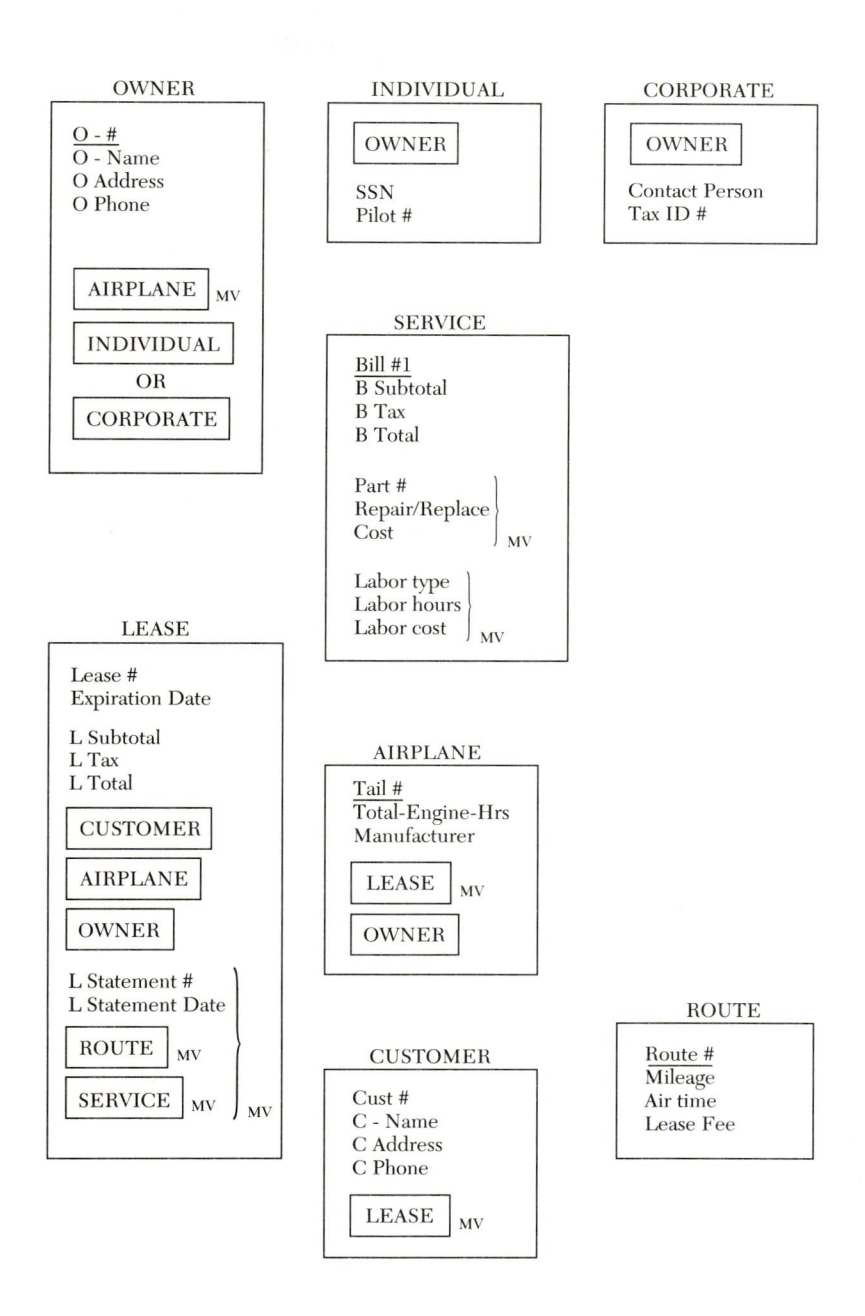

[AIRPLANE] MV

[INDIVIDUAL]
OR
[CORPORATE]

INDIVIDUAL
[OWNER]
- SSN
- Pilot #

CORPORATE
[OWNER]
- Contact Person
- Tax ID #

SERVICE
- Bill #1
- B Subtotal
- B Tax
- B Total

- Part #
- Repair/Replace
- Cost } MV

- Labor type
- Labor hours
- Labor cost } MV

LEASE
- Lease #
- Expiration Date
- L Subtotal
- L Tax
- L Total

[CUSTOMER]
[AIRPLANE]
[OWNER]

- L Statement #
- L Statement Date
- [ROUTE] MV
- [SERVICE] MV } MV

AIRPLANE
- Tail #
- Total-Engine-Hrs
- Manufacturer

[LEASE] MV
[OWNER]

CUSTOMER
- Cust #
- C - Name
- C Address
- C Phone

[LEASE] MV

ROUTE
- Route #
- Mileage
- Air time
- Lease Fee

FIGURE 1

Figure 2 is an example of a simple object, SCHOOL SUPPLIES:

SCHOOL SUPPLIES			
Supply #	Supply Desc	Purchase Date	Purchase Price

FIGURE 2

76   Case 11 - Transforming a Semantic Object Data Model

      (a)   Diagram ROUTE like the example SCHOOL SUPPLIES.

3. The next object to transform is the composite object of SERVICE.
   (a) How many relations will you need to transform this object?
   (b) Why do you need this many?
   (c) What are the keys for the composite groups?
   (d) Diagram the relations.

4. Next you will transform into relations the special case of the compound objects: association objects.
   (a) Pattern the association object transformation of PILOT, AIRPLANE, and FLIGHT after the general transformation in Figure 3. Include only the relations pertaining to the association part of the objects.

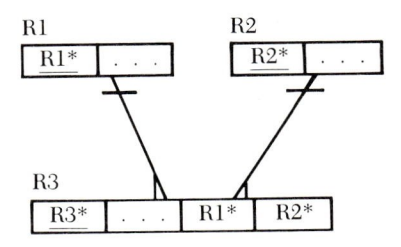

```
        R1                    R2
     ┌──────┬───┐          ┌──────┬───┐
     │ R1*  │...│          │ R2*  │...│
     └──────┴───┘          └──────┴───┘
            \                 /
             \               /
              \             /
        R3     \           /
     ┌──────┬───┬──────┬──────┐
     │ R3*  │...│ R1*  │ R2*  │
     └──────┴───┴──────┴──────┘

              Relational representation
```

FIGURE 3

5. The next step is to transform the generalization hierarchy of OWNER. Figure 4 shows an example of a generalization hierarchy of an object, TRIP.

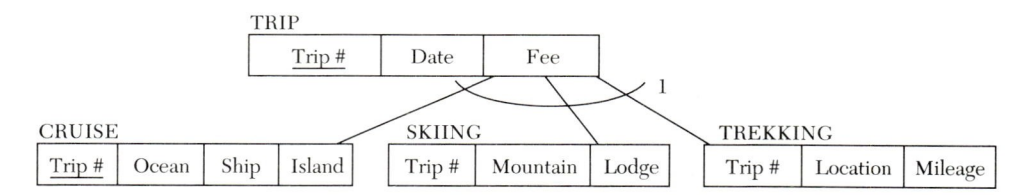

```
                    TRIP
              ┌───────┬──────┬─────┐
              │ Trip #│ Date │ Fee │
              └───────┴──────┴─────┘
                                          1
   CRUISE                SKIING                 TREKKING
 ┌──────┬─────┬─────┬──────┐ ┌──────┬────────┬───────┐ ┌──────┬─────────┬─────────┐
 │Trip #│Ocean│Ship │Island│ │Trip #│Mountain│ Lodge │ │Trip #│Location │ Mileage │
 └──────┴─────┴─────┴──────┘ └──────┴────────┴───────┘ └──────┴─────────┴─────────┘
```

FIGURE 4

      The curved line designates the subtypes and the 1 means the trips are mutually exclusive.

      (a)   Diagram the OWNER generalization hierarchy. Leave out the LEASE and AIRPLANE objects in OWNER.

6. Look at the association relation you developed in Question #5.
   (a) Is the AIRPLANE relation complete in its transformation?
   (b) Is the CUSTOMER relation complete in its transformation?
   (c) LEASE is a hybrid object. How many relations are in its transformation? Diagram the composite group part of the relation.

Case 11 - Transforming a Semantic Object Data Model

7. You now have relations representing every semantic object. Evaluate the relations for normalization criteria. Explain how the relations meet normalization criteria or explain the changes you made.

8. The next step is creating a data structure diagram. Since most of the objects are connected to LEASE, put the LEASE relation in the middle of the page. Then connect AIRPLANE, CUSTOMER, and OWNER to LEASE. Finish by connecting the subtypes to OWNER and OWNER to AIRPLANE.

This will complete your data structure diagram. The final phase of the development process is implementation. The primary task of implementation is to construct the system according to the design. Hardware is installed, programs are developed, procedures are documented, and personnel are hired and trained.

CASE 12
PARTIAL IMPLEMENTATION OF A RELATIONAL DATABASE DESIGN

You have learned the essential skill of creating a DBMS-independent data structure design. Now you must learn the rules of the DBMS so you can implement the database for the user.

In cases 10 and 11 you created DBMS-independent data structure designs using the relational model. The next step is to implement the database using a DBMS. This case uses the DBMS of Paradox. If you are using a different DBMS, you can still complete this case. You will follow the sequence of implementation steps, but disregard the instructions specific to the Paradox software.

Even though Paradox is designed for the relational data model, you will need to modify the data structure diagrams you developed in order to use them with Paradox. The relational model cannot be implemented exactly as it is because of the rules of the Paradox software. Most of the changes are needed to improve the speed of processing.

Specifically, in this case you will:
- Create tables
- Create a standard form
- Create a standard report
- See how the parts of a partial implementation work together

For this case study you will create a form and a report about the sales managers at the airplane dealership franchises. At headquarters in Skagit Valley, the office manager needs an easy way to enter data about the sales manager at each franchise. She also wants a simple report that lists the sales manager's name and address and the franchise's name. You will use the FRANCHISE and SALESPERSON relations you developed in Case 10. To complete the questions in this case, we have made two assumptions for you. The first one is that the attributes of SALESPERSON and SALES MANAGER are the same. The second assumption is that there is a 1:1 relationship between SALES MANAGER and FRANCHISE. In this partial implementation, you will create tables for SALES MANAGER and FRANCHISE, create a source table and a map table to enter data and then create a standard form and a report from the source table.

Questions for the Partial Implementation Plan
1. The first step is to define the tables. The first table you will create is C12-fr (for the FRANCHISE relation).

   These are the attributes in the FRANCHISE relation from Case 10:
   Franchise #, Name, Address, Phone

   This relation needs to be changed slightly to convert it to a Paradox table. The Address attribute has to be expanded to the four fields of Address, City, State, and Zip. Paradox can then manipulate the fields separately. Rename the Name attribute to Franchise Name, so it has a distinct field name.

   > *Create the C12-fam table with the fields* Franchise #, Franchise Name, Address, City, State, Zip, and Phone. Use appropriate field types and designate the Franchise # field as a key.

Case 12 - Partial Implementation of a Relational Database Design   79

2. Next, you will create the C12-sm table. The attributes in the SALESPERSON relation from Case 10 are *Salesperson #*, Name, Address, Phone, and *Franchise #*. In the C12-sm table, the key, *Salesperson #*, should be renamed Sales Manager #. Move the attribute Franchise # to the beginning of the relation. Because Franchise # is a foreign key, it has to be a keyed field in the C12-fam table. When you move Franchise #, you change the data structure design to a DBMS-dependent design. Paradox requires that all keyed fields are the first fields in the tables.

    The attributes of Name and Address must be split into separate parts and each part given a field name. The separate fields allow Paradox to manipulate the data independently. For the Name attribute, use the field names Title, Fname, and Lname. For the Address attribute, use the fields Address, City, State, and Zip. Use data definitions you think are reasonable. Remember to put an asterisk beside the key fields.

    > Create table C12-sm. Franchise # and Sales Manager # are the key fields. The other fields are Title, Fname, Lname, Address, City, State, Zip, and Phone. Use appropriate field types.

3. Now that you have the tables set up, the next step is to enter data into them. Paradox's default data entry method is to enter the data directly into the tables. This is not easy for users because the tables do not look like forms. You will use Paradox's standard form to enter data.

    If you had a copy of a form the user wanted to continue using, you could create a standard form similar to it on the screen. Since you don't have a form, you need to think about the entities in the user's environment. When the office manager thinks of a sales manager at a franchise, she probably thinks of the FRANCHISE object first and then the SALES MANAGER object. To create a standard form with the FRANCHISE information first and the SALES MANAGER information second, you can create a source table. The user enters data into the source table, so it is the source of the user's information. The source table has target tables, which in this case are C12-fr and C12-sm. Associated with every source table is a map table. The map table tells the source table where to put the information in the target tables. It isn't as complicated as it sounds. The first step is to construct the source table as if you were constructing an answer table. You need to create a query in the workspace that represents the source table.

    > **F10|Ask|Select C12-fr|** Check and put an example element in the Franchise # field and check the Franchise Name field. We won't use the rest of the fields for this data entry form and report.
    > **F10|Ask|Select C12-sm|** Put the same example element in the Franchise # field and check the rest of the fields. Do **not** press F2.

4. The next step is to create the source table and the map. With the query tables on the screen, you will create the source table.

> **F10|Modify|MultiEntry|SetUp.** Pick a name for your source table and press **Enter.**
> The top line changes to "Map name:". Pick a name for your map table and press **Enter.**

Check the map table to see if the fields in the source table are correctly filling the target tables. Use the right arrow key to see the last field of the map table. The Source Field is a list of the fields in C12-sm and C12-fr. The Target Field is the same as the Source Field. The Target Table field should show that each field is filling the table it belongs to. Franchise # should be shown filling the C12-sm and the C12-fr tables.

5. You will use Paradox's standard form to enter data into the source table you created. These are the commands to bring up the standard form:

> **Alt F8|Modify|MultiEntry|Entry|Type in source table name|Enter|**
> Type in map table name|Enter
> The entry table will appear on the screen. To bring up the form, press **F7.**

6. The purpose of the standard form is to make it easy for the user to input data. Use your form to input at least five records. Remember that the Franchise # and Sales Manager # are key fields, so the entries must be unique. Use the Enter key and the up and down arrow keys to move between fields in the form. Use the backspace key to correct typing errors. When you are finished entering the records, press **F2**.

7. The office manager wants to print out a listing of sales managers with their addresses and phone numbers. You will use Paradox's standard report function to create this report. The standard report lists the information in tabular form with the field names as headings. These are the commands to produce the standard report:

> **F10|Report|Enter (Output)|Type C12-sm|Enter|Enter (Standard report)|Enter (Printer)**

As you can see, the process of implementation is very involved for even a simple data entry form and standard report. That's why the field of database design and processing is so fascinating—it involves fitting all the pieces together so that the whole system works.

STANDARD REPORTS

8/22/91   Standard Report   Page 1

JOB#	C#	JOB TITLE	JOB DESCRIPTION	SALARY
10	500	ACCOUNTANT	ASSISTANT TO CONTROLLER	35,000.00
20	400	INFORMATION SYSTEMS SPECIALIST	INTERNAL CONSULTANT	55,000.00
30	485	HUMAN RESOURCE SPECIALIST	INTERNAL CONSULTANT	40,000.00
40	450	ACCOUNTANT	SALES REPRESENTATIVE	30,000.00
50	415	HUMAN RESOURCE SPECIALIST	TRAINER	35,000.00
60	425	ACCOUNTANT	MANAGEMENT TRAINEE	32,000.00
70	475	INFORMATION SYSTEMS SPECIALIST	DATABASE ADMINISTRATOR	47,000.00

Field Name	Field Type
Job #	N°
C #	N°
Job Title	A30
Job Description	A25
Salary	$

C1-Job

8/22/91   Standard Report   Page 1

C#	BUSINESS DESCRIPTION	# EMP	ANNUAL REV	INTERNATIONAL
400	MFG	900	95,000,000.00	Y
415	SERVICE	10000	5,000,000.00	N
425	SERVICE	1000	1,000,000.00	N
450	SOFTWARE DEV	500	5,000,000.00	Y
475	INSURANCE	50000	50,000,000.00	N
485	RETAIL	20000	25,000,000.00	N
500	MFG	5000	10,000,000.00	Y

Field Name	Field Type
C#	N°
Business Description	A12
# EMP	N
Annual Rev	$
International	A1

C1-Com

Standard Reports

8/22/91   Standard Report   Page 1

CHARTER#	CHARTER NAME	PRICE	DEPARTURE DATE	RETURN DATE
1500	ASIA EXPRESS	450.00	7/01/93	10/01/93
1689	HIFYING	600.00	6/15/93	6/25/93
1742	ASIA EXPRESS	600.00	6/05/93	9/20/93
1880	TOP FLYERS	400.00	6/10/93	7/02/93
1892	ASIA EXPRESS	550.00	6/01/93	8/01/93
1990	HIFYING	900.00	6/01/93	7/01/93

Field Name	Field Type
Charter #	N°
Charter Name	A15
Price	$
Departure Date	D
Return Date	D

C7-Chart

8/22/91   Standard Report   Page 1

Country Name	Climate	Charter #
BALI	TROPICAL	1892
NEPAL	MOUNTAINOUS	1689
SINGAPORE	TROPICAL	1500
SWITZERLAND	MOUNTAINOUS	1880
THAILAND	TROPICAL	1742
TIBET	MOUNTAINOUS	1990

Field Name	Field Type
Country Name	A20°
Climate	A20
Charter #	N

C7-Cntry

ANSWERS

(CASES 2–6)

CASE 2

1. (a) EMPLOYEE, OFFICE MANAGER, COOK/MAINTENANCE PERSON, SKI INSTRUCTOR, APPRENTICE, TOUR GUIDE, BEGINNING SKI COURSE, TOUR, CUSTOMER, EQUIPMENT

2. (a)
   SKI INSTRUCTOR
   Social Security Number
   Name
   Address
   City
   State
   Zip
   Phone #
   Per Diem Rate ($/day)
   Assignment

   BEGINNING SKI COURSE
   Course #
   Customer - 10
   Ski Instructor - 2
   Apprentice - 1
   Tour Guide - 2
   Equipment MV
   Fee

   CUSTOMER
   Customer #
   Customer Name
   Address
   City
   State
   Zip
   Phone #
   Courses Taken MV
   Equipment Bought MV

3. SKI INSTRUCTOR Instance
   546-82-5920
   Debbie Church
   478 Willow Road
   George
   WA
   98788
   (206) 789-4926
   75
   Course 23

Answers - Case 2

BEGINNING SKI COURSE Instance
Course 23
Joe Iena, Connie Chung, Fred Kowlinski, Phil McGhowan, Nancy Beoli, Judy Frederick, Tran Phong, Amy Heller, Howard Isherbaum, Lois Takoto
Debbie Church, Sandra Adler
John Gothward
Bill James, Audrey Svitha
S10, S11, S45, S67, B34, B45, B56, B57, P1, P2, P16, P17
889

CUSTOMER Instance
2345
Sharon Hill
23 Independence Lane
Preston
WA
98056
(206) 566-3452
Beginning Ski Course, Tour
Skis, Boots, Poles

4. (a) 1:1, 1:N, N:M

5. (a) 1:1 BEGINNING SKI COURSE to APPRENTICE
    1:N BEGINNING SKI COURSE to SKI INSTRUCTOR
    N:M CUSTOMER to EQUIPMENT

   (b) They are all HAS-A relationships.

6. (a) An entity whose existence depends on the existence of another entity is a weak entity.
   (b) ID-dependent entities
   (c) No
   (d) Weak entity: A situation could be that each TOUR has a specific ROUTE. A route can physically exist even if a tour does not use it and would probably have an identifier Route #.

   ID-dependent entity: A situation could be that each piece of EQUIPMENT has a PREVENTATIVE MAINTENANCE TIME SLOT. The existence of PREVENTATIVE MAINTENANCE TIME SLOT is dependent on the EQUIPMENT existing. Its identifier is the group (*Serial #, Date, Time*), which includes the EQUIPMENT identifier *Serial #*.

7. (a) Generalization hierarchies are structures in which one supertype entity is a generalization of subtypes.
   (b) EMPLOYEE is a supertype with subtypes of INSTRUCTOR, OFFICE MANAGER, COOK/MAINTENANCE PERSON; INSTRUCTOR is a supertype with subtypes of SKI INSTRUCTOR, APPRENTICE, AND TOUR GUIDE.

8. (a) Recursive relationships are relationships among entities of a single class.
   (b) If ski instructors trained other ski instructors on new routes or new equipment, then the relationship would be among entities of a single class.

Answers - Case 2

Part 2

9.

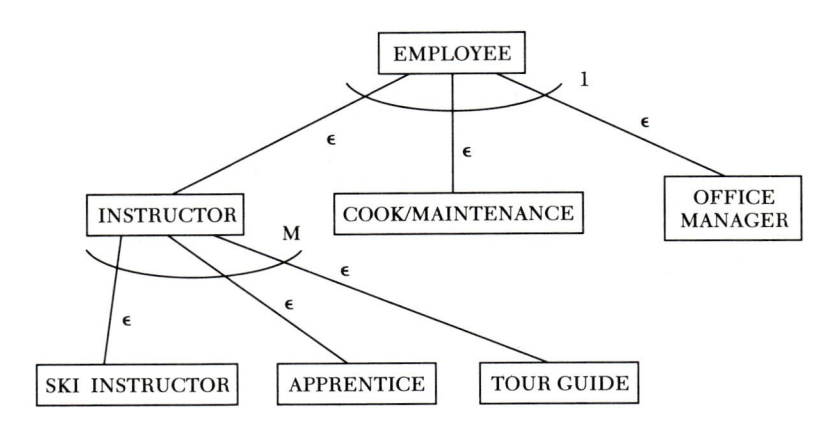

```
                    EMPLOYEE
           ε     ε     1    ε
      INSTRUCTOR  COOK/MAINTENANCE  OFFICE MANAGER
         M
    ε    ε      ε
  SKI INSTRUCTOR   APPRENTICE   TOUR GUIDE
```

Answer Diagram #1

10.

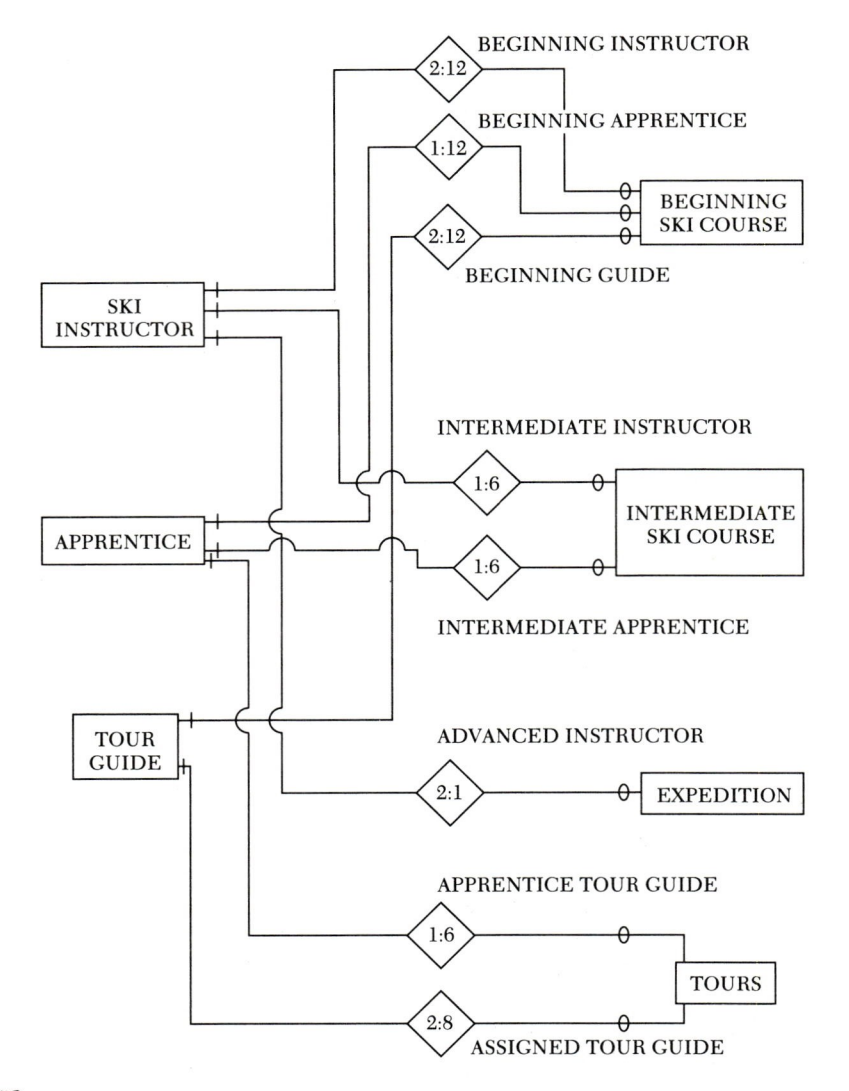

```
                                    BEGINNING INSTRUCTOR
                              ⟨2:12⟩
                                    BEGINNING APPRENTICE
                              ⟨1:12⟩                        BEGINNING
                                                            SKI COURSE
                              ⟨2:12⟩
                                    BEGINNING GUIDE
   SKI
   INSTRUCTOR

                                    INTERMEDIATE INSTRUCTOR
                              ⟨1:6⟩
                                                            INTERMEDIATE
                                                            SKI COURSE
                              ⟨1:6⟩
   APPRENTICE                       INTERMEDIATE APPRENTICE


                                    ADVANCED INSTRUCTOR
   TOUR
   GUIDE                      ⟨2:1⟩                          EXPEDITION

                                    APPRENTICE TOUR GUIDE
                              ⟨1:6⟩
                                                              TOURS
                              ⟨2:8⟩
                                    ASSIGNED TOUR GUIDE
```

Answer Diagram #2

Answers - Case 2

11.

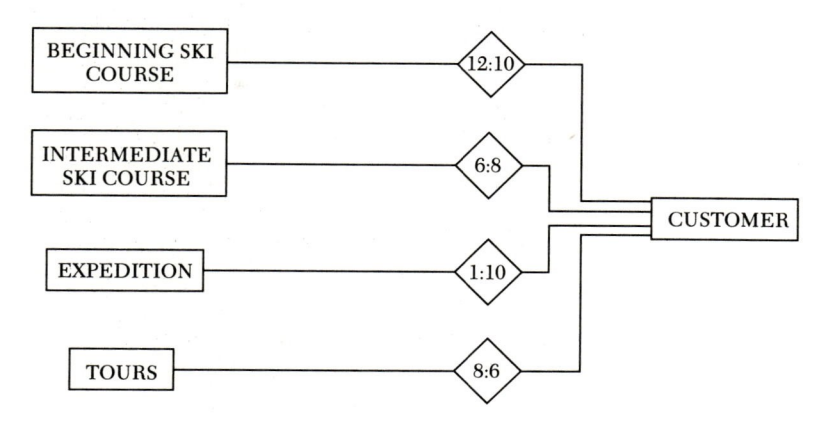

```
BEGINNING SKI COURSE ──── <12:10> ────┐
                                       │
INTERMEDIATE SKI COURSE ──── <6:8> ────┤
                                       ├──── CUSTOMER
EXPEDITION ──── <1:10> ────────────────┤
                                       │
TOURS ──── <8:6> ──────────────────────┘
```

Answer Diagram #3

12. (a) CONTACT is an ID-dependent weak entity.
    (b)

```
                    CUSTOMER
                    CONTACT
                      LIST
    CUSTOMER ────── <1:N> ────── CONTACT
```

Answer Diagram #4

13. RENTAL EQUIPMENT, SALES ORDER, PURCHASE ORDER, MERCHANDISE INVENTORY, SUPPLIER

14.

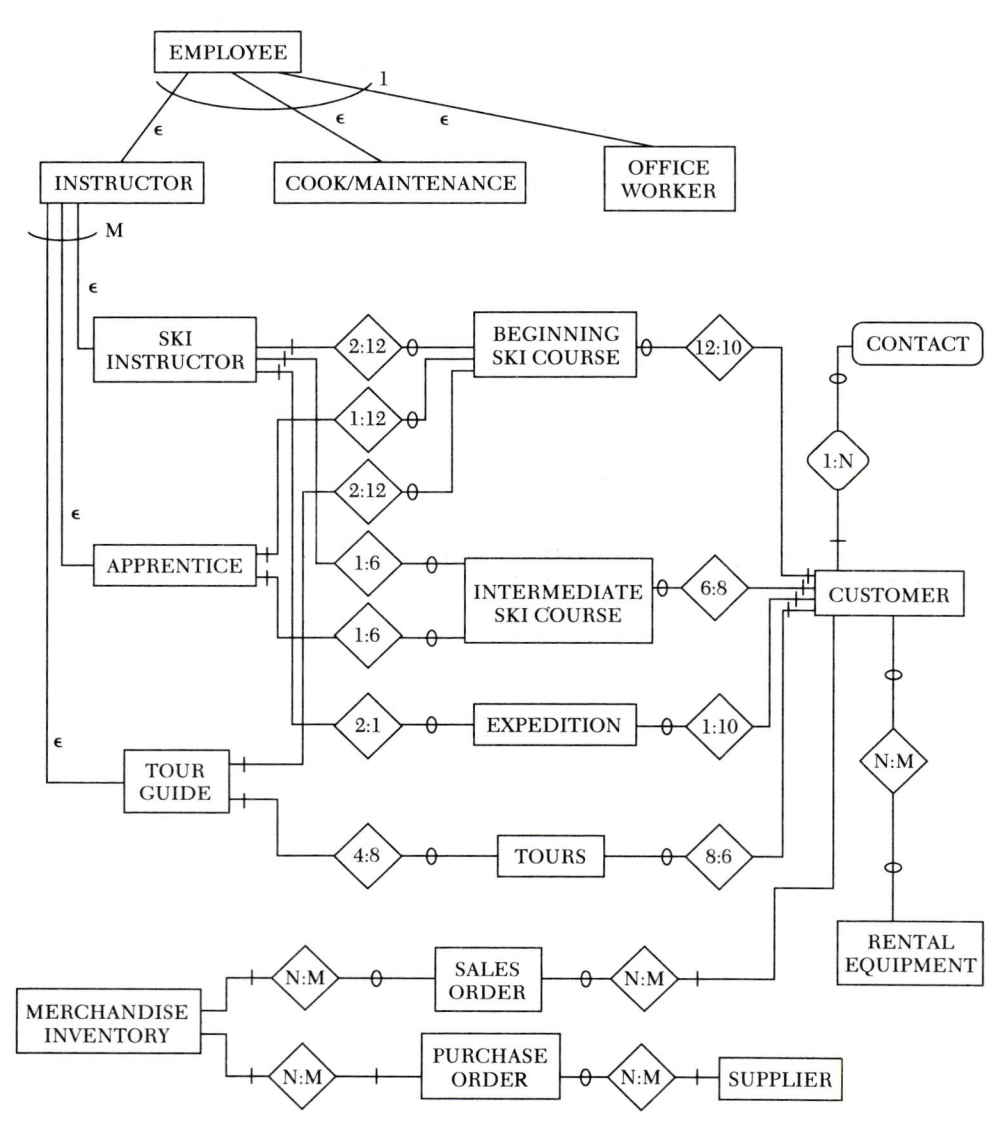

Answer Diagram #5

15. (a) INSTRUCTOR
       Additions Processing Restriction
       Before INSTRUCTOR data can be added, EMPLOYEE data must be added.
    (b) INSTRUCTOR
       Changes Processing Restriction
       If any of the properties of INSTRUCTOR have been propagated to other entities, then changes to INSTRUCTOR must be made to the propagated properties.
    (c) CUSTOMER
       Deletion Processing Restriction
       Before a CUSTOMER instance can be deleted, any CONTACTS instances related to that CUSTOMER must be deleted.

Answers - Case 2

16. **Question 1**

    How are the instructors, apprentices, and tour guides assigned? The E-R model shows the relationships between the subtypes of INSTRUCTOR and the courses, expedition, and tours.

    Question 2

    Which customer has which rental equipment? The E-R model shows a many to many relationship between CUSTOMER and RENTAL EQUIPMENT.

    Question 3

    What is on order for the retail business? The E-R model shows a many to many relationship between the MERCHANDISE INVENTORY and PURCHASE ORDER.

CASE 3

Part 1
1. (a) COURSE
   (b) INSTRUCTOR. The relationship between COURSE and INSTRUCTOR is a 1:N relationship.
   (c)

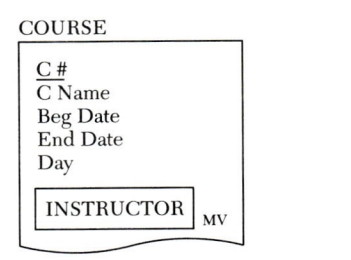

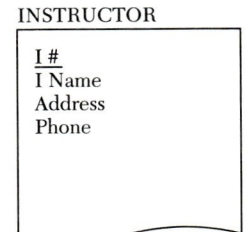

```
COURSE                          INSTRUCTOR
┌─────────────┐                 ┌─────────────┐
│ C #         │                 │ I #         │
│ C Name      │                 │ I Name      │
│ Beg Date    │                 │ Address     │
│ End Date    │                 │ Phone       │
│ Day         │                 │             │
│ ┌─────────┐ │                 │             │
│ │INSTRUCTOR│MV│               │             │
│ └─────────┘ │                 │             │
```

Answer Diagram #1

2. (a) There is a 1:N relationship between INSTRUCTOR and EQUIPMENT.
   (b)

```
       INSTRUCTOR
       ┌─────────────┐
       │ I #         │
       │ I Name      │
       │ Address     │
       │ Phone       │
       │ ┌─────────┐ │
       │ │EQUIPMENT│MV│
       │ └─────────┘ │
```

Answer Diagram #2

   (c) Yes, it will have INSTRUCTOR in it. The screen shows EQUIPMENT identified with a specific instructor.

```
       EQUIPMENT
       ┌──────────────────┐
       │ E #              │
       │ Equip Description│
       │ Condition        │
       │ ┌──────────┐     │
       │ │INSTRUCTOR│     │
       │ └──────────┘     │
```

Answer Diagram #3

Case 3 - Answers

3. (a) It is about the object INSTRUCTOR and another object, STUDENT. INSTRUCTOR has a 1:N relationship to STUDENT and EQUIPMENT.
   (b)

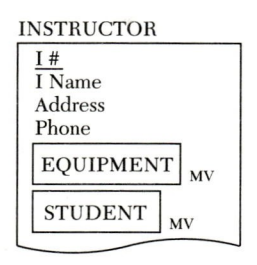

   INSTRUCTOR
   - I #
   - I Name
   - Address
   - Phone
   - EQUIPMENT MV
   - STUDENT MV

   STUDENT
   - S #
   - S Name
   - Address
   - Phone
   - INSTRUCTOR

Answer Diagram #4

4. (a) One piece of equipment can be associated with many students and many instructors.
   (b)

   EQUIPMENT
   - E#
   - Equip Description
   - Condition
   - INSTRUCTOR MV
   - STUDENT MV

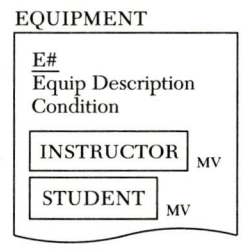

Answer Diagram #5

   (c)

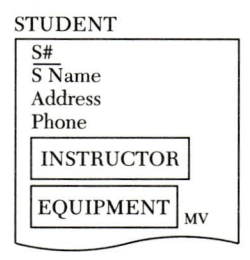

   STUDENT
   - S#
   - S Name
   - Address
   - Phone
   - INSTRUCTOR
   - EQUIPMENT MV

Answer Diagram #6

5. (a) STUDENT LIST
   (b) *Directory #*, Date, COURSE, STUDENT
   (c)

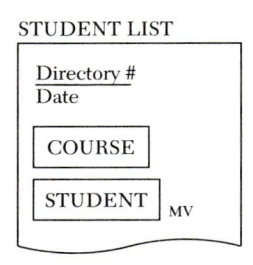

```
            STUDENT LIST
         ┌─────────────────┐
         │ Directory #     │
         │ Date            │
         │  ┌────────┐     │
         │  │ COURSE │     │
         │  └────────┘     │
         │  ┌─────────┐    │
         │  │ STUDENT │ MV │
         │  └─────────┘    │
         └─────────────────┘
```

Answer Diagram #7

6.

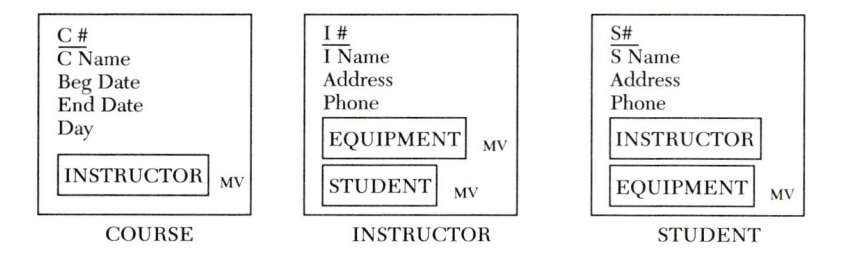

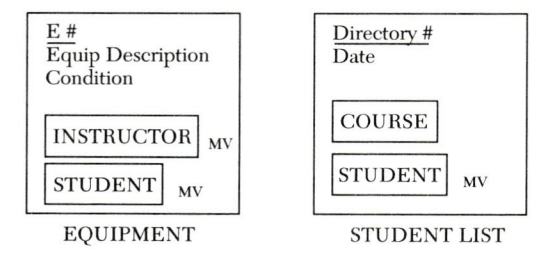

```
┌──────────────────┐    ┌──────────────────┐    ┌──────────────────┐
│ C #              │    │ I #              │    │ S #              │
│ C Name           │    │ I Name           │    │ S Name           │
│ Beg Date         │    │ Address          │    │ Address          │
│ End Date         │    │ Phone            │    │ Phone            │
│ Day              │    │ ┌───────────┐    │    │ ┌────────────┐   │
│ ┌────────────┐   │    │ │ EQUIPMENT │ MV │    │ │ INSTRUCTOR │ MV│
│ │ INSTRUCTOR │MV │    │ └───────────┘    │    │ └────────────┘   │
│ └────────────┘   │    │ ┌─────────┐      │    │ ┌───────────┐    │
└──────────────────┘    │ │ STUDENT │ MV   │    │ │ EQUIPMENT │ MV │
      COURSE            │ └─────────┘      │    │ └───────────┘    │
                        └──────────────────┘    └──────────────────┘
                              INSTRUCTOR               STUDENT


┌────────────────────┐    ┌─────────────────┐
│ E #                │    │ Directory #     │
│ Equip Description  │    │ Date            │
│ Condition          │    │ ┌────────┐      │
│ ┌────────────┐     │    │ │ COURSE │      │
│ │ INSTRUCTOR │ MV  │    │ └────────┘      │
│ └────────────┘     │    │ ┌─────────┐     │
│ ┌─────────┐        │    │ │ STUDENT │ MV  │
│ │ STUDENT │ MV     │    │ └─────────┘     │
│ └─────────┘        │    └─────────────────┘
└────────────────────┘        STUDENT LIST
     EQUIPMENT
```

Answer Diagram #8

Part 2

7. The objects are compound objects. Compound objects are frequently used objects, and the screens are similar in format.

Case 3 - Answers

8. (a) This is a simple form. The properties are single-valued and non-object properties.
   (b)

```
┌─────────────────────────┐
│                         │
│   Trail Name            │
│   Skill Level           │
│   Total Length          │
│   Total Elevation Gain  │
│   Grooming Status       │
│   Description           │
│                         │
└─────────────────────────┘
          TRAIL
```

Answer Diagram #9

9. (a) Package Name, Item Description, Item Subtotal, Subtotal, Tax, and Total Order
   (b) Features is multivalued and the composite group of Item Description, Features, and Item Subtotal is multivalued.
   (c) PACKAGE is a composite object.
   (d)

```
┌─────────────────────────┐
│                         │
│   P Name                │
│   Subtotal              │
│   Tax                   │
│   Total                 │
│                         │
│   Item Description  ⎫   │
│   Features MV       ⎬ MV│
│   Item Subtotal     ⎭   │
│                         │
└─────────────────────────┘
         PACKAGE
```

Answer Diagram #10

10. There are nine subtypes of compound objects. Three are represented in Part 1:
    Object 1 can contain one; Object 2 can contain many
    (STUDENT to INSTRUCTOR)
    Object 1 can contain many; Object 2 can contain many
    (INSTRUCTOR to EQUIPMENT)
    Object 1 can contain many; Object 2 can contain unknown
    (COURSE to INSTRUCTOR)

96   Case 3 - Answers

11. (a) Association object
    (b)

```
┌─────────────────┐   ┌─────────────────┐   ┌─────────────────┐
│ Lesson #        │   │ I #             │   │ S#              │
│ Date            │   │ I Name          │   │ S Name          │
│ Time            │   │ Address         │   │ Address         │
│ Fee             │   │ Phone           │   │ Phone           │
│ ┌────────────┐  │   │                 │   │                 │
│ │ INSTRUCTOR │  │   │ ┌──────────────┐│   │ ┌────────────┐  │
│ └────────────┘  │   │ │PRIVATE LESSON│MV  │ │ INSTRUCTOR │MV│
│ ┌────────────┐  │   │ └──────────────┘│   │ └────────────┘  │
│ │  STUDENT   │  │   │                 │   │                 │
│ └────────────┘  │   │                 │   │                 │
└─────────────────┘   └─────────────────┘   └─────────────────┘
  PRIVATE LESSON           INSTRUCTOR             STUDENT
```

Answer Diagram #11

12. (a) Hybrid object
    (b)

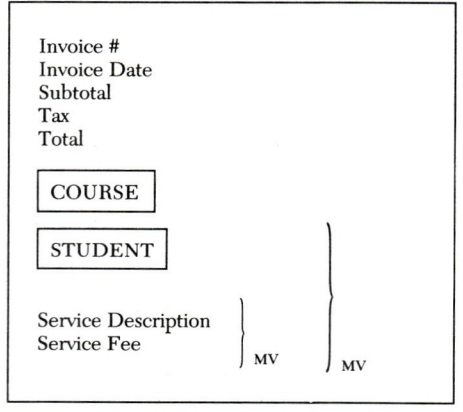

```
┌──────────────────────────────────┐
│ Invoice #                        │
│ Invoice Date                     │
│ Subtotal                         │
│ Tax                              │
│ Total                            │
│ ┌─────────┐                      │
│ │ COURSE  │                      │
│ └─────────┘                      │
│ ┌─────────┐                      │
│ │ STUDENT │                      │
│ └─────────┘                      │
│                                  │
│ Service Description  ⎫    ⎫      │
│ Service Fee          ⎬ MV ⎬ MV   │
│                      ⎭    ⎭      │
└──────────────────────────────────┘
           RESORT INVOICE
```

Answer Diagram #12

   (c) Answers will vary according to the students' examples.
   (d) An example of the object specification and domain definitions:

Object Specification

   RESORT INVOICE OBJECT

   Invoice #: Invoice numbers
   Invoice Date: Dates
   Subtotal: Currency
   Tax: Currency
   Total: Currency
   Service Description: Designated service descriptions
   Service Fee: Currency

Case 3 - Answers

Domain Definitions

Currency:
    Currency format
    U.S. currency
Dates:
    Date format
    Dates from the establishment date of Northern Star Expeditions (9/1/78) to current date
Invoice numbers:
    Numeric
    Unique number on invoice
Service Description:
    Text 30
    Designated service descriptions
Service Fee:
    Currency format
    U.S. currency

13.

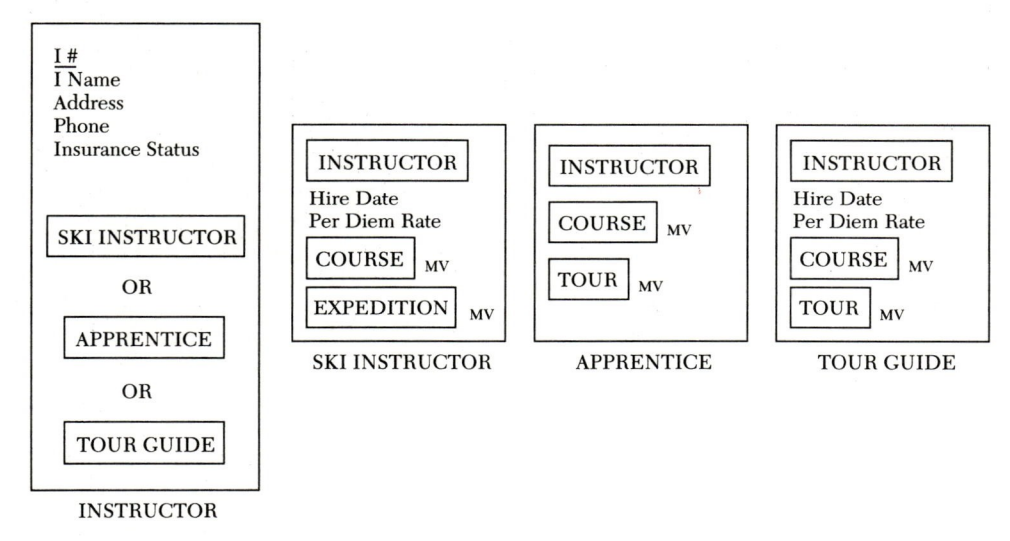

INSTRUCTOR
- I #
- I Name
- Address
- Phone
- Insurance Status

SKI INSTRUCTOR
OR
APPRENTICE
OR
TOUR GUIDE

SKI INSTRUCTOR
- INSTRUCTOR
- Hire Date
- Per Diem Rate
- COURSE (MV)
- EXPEDITION (MV)

APPRENTICE
- INSTRUCTOR
- COURSE (MV)
- TOUR (MV)

TOUR GUIDE
- INSTRUCTOR
- Hire Date
- Per Diem Rate
- COURSE (MV)
- TOUR (MV)

Answer Diagram #13

CASE 4

1. (a) FAMILY PLAN (<u>Plan #</u>, Number in family, Expiration date)
   CUSTOMER (<u>Cust #</u>, Name, Address)
   PASSES (<u>Pass #</u>, Fee, Expiration date)
   EQUIPMENT (<u>Serial #</u>, Description, Purchase date)
   CONTACTS (<u>Cust #</u>, <u>Contacts</u>, Date Sent, Response Date, Coupon #)
   SURVEYS (<u>Cust #</u>, <u>Contact #</u>, Description)
   UPGRADES (<u>Cust #</u>, Contact #, Equip Description)
   REGS (<u>Cust #</u>, Contact #, Course Description)
   CLASS (<u>Class #</u>, Cname, Location , Beg Date, Fee)
   BEG (<u>Class #</u>, Permit #, Rental #)
   INT (<u>Class #</u>, Int Permit #, Int Contract #)
   TEL (<u>Class #</u>, Class Lift Ticket #, Class Lift Ticket Fee)
   EXP (<u>Class #</u>, Travel Packet #, Travel Agent Name)

   (b) Each answer is specific to the student's choice of attributes. With the stipulation of only two non-key attributes, most relations will be in DK/NF.

2. FAMILY PLAN (<u>Plan #</u>, Number in family, Expiration date, *Cust #*)

3. The key of the parent relation must be placed in the child relation.
   PASSES (<u>Pass #</u>, Fee, Expiration date, *Cust #*)

4. The similarity is that they are both 1:N binary relationships. The difference is that CONTACTS is an ID-dependent weak entity, so it already has the key of its parent in the relation.

5. (a) Create an intersection table.
   (b) CUST-EQUIP (<u>Cust #</u>, <u>Serial #</u>)
       CUST-CLASS (<u>Cust #</u>, <u>Class #</u>)

6. This is a 1:N recursive relationship. The CUSTOMER relation needs a new attribute of Referred-by.
   CUSTOMER (<u>Cust #</u>, Name, Address, Referred-by)

7. The relations in Question #1 show the key of the generalization relation as the key of the subtype. None of the subtypes have their own keys.

Case 4 - Answers

8. This diagram will answer the rest of the questions (9–12).

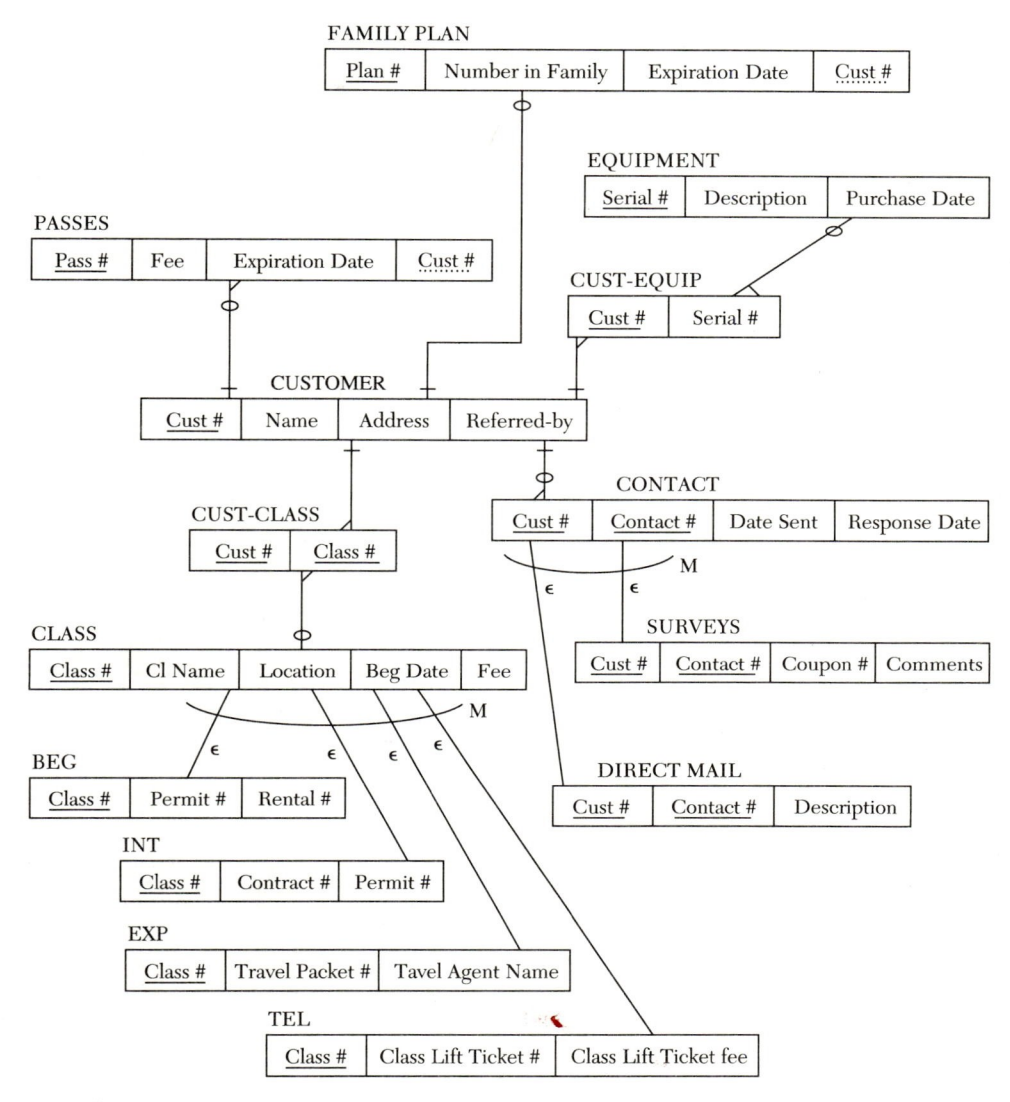

FAMILY PLAN

| Plan # | Number in Family | Expiration Date | Cust # |

EQUIPMENT

| Serial # | Description | Purchase Date |

PASSES

| Pass # | Fee | Expiration Date | Cust # |

CUST-EQUIP

| Cust # | Serial # |

CUSTOMER

| Cust # | Name | Address | Referred-by |

CONTACT

| Cust # | Contact # | Date Sent | Response Date |

CUST-CLASS

| Cust # | Class # |

SURVEYS

| Cust # | Contact # | Coupon # | Comments |

CLASS

| Class # | Cl Name | Location | Beg Date | Fee |

DIRECT MAIL

| Cust # | Contact # | Description |

BEG

| Class # | Permit # | Rental # |

INT

| Class # | Contract # | Permit # |

EXP

| Class # | Travel Packet # | Tavel Agent Name |

TEL

| Class # | Class Lift Ticket # | Class Lift Ticket fee |

Answer Diagram #1

9. See answer for #8

10. See answer for #8

11. See answer for #8

12. See answer for #8

CASE 5

1. Simple object: ITEM
   Composite object: SHIPPING COST
   Compound object: SALESPERSON, CUSTOMER, EQUIPMENT DM
   Association object: SALESPERSON, ORDER, CUSTOMER
   Hybrid object: ORDER
   Generalization hierarchy: DIRECT MAIL (supertype),
   COURSE DM, EQUIPMENT DM, and COMBINED DM (subtypes)

2.

   ITEM

I #	I Desc	Manufacturer	Supplier	Unit Price

Answer Diagram #1

3. (a) 2
   (b) You need one for the object SHIPPING COST and one for the composite group.
   (c) It is a composite key of Shipping #, Service Description.
   (d)

   SHIPPING COST

Shipping #	Date	Weight	Region	Size

Shipping #	Service Desc	Pkg Material	Pkg Labor	Pkg Fee

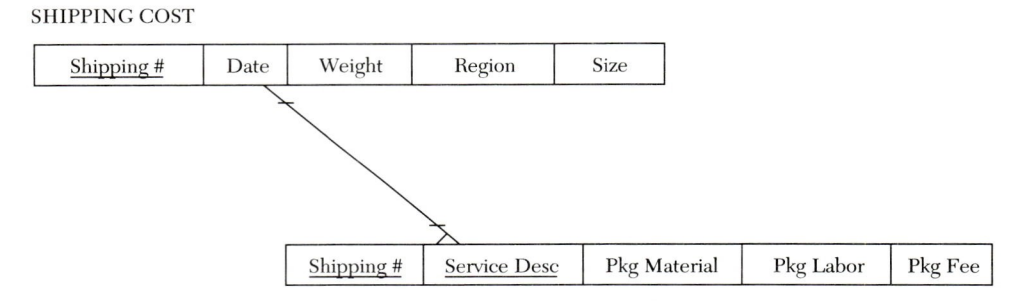

Answer Diagram #2

4.

   CUSTOMER

C#	C Name	C Address	C Phone

   SALESPERSON

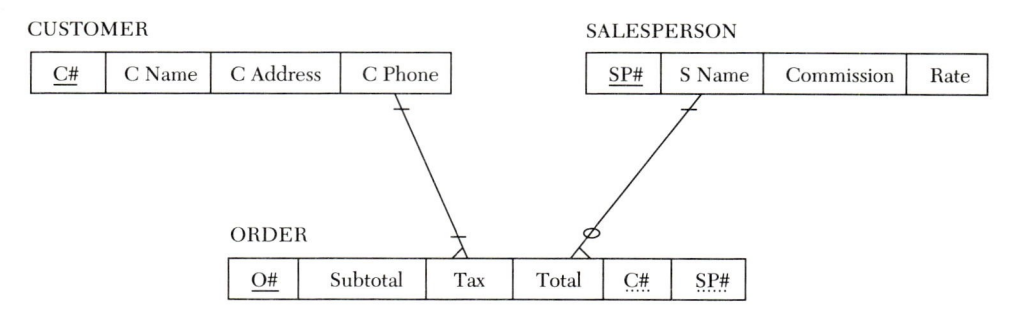

SP#	S Name	Commission	Rate

   ORDER

O#	Subtotal	Tax	Total	C#	SP#

Answer Diagram #3

Case 5 - Answers

5.

DIRECT MAIL

Piece #	Date Sent

COURSE DM

Piece #	Course #	Course Name	Course Desc	Fee

EQUIPMENT DM

Piece #	Package Price	Offer End Date

COMBINED DM

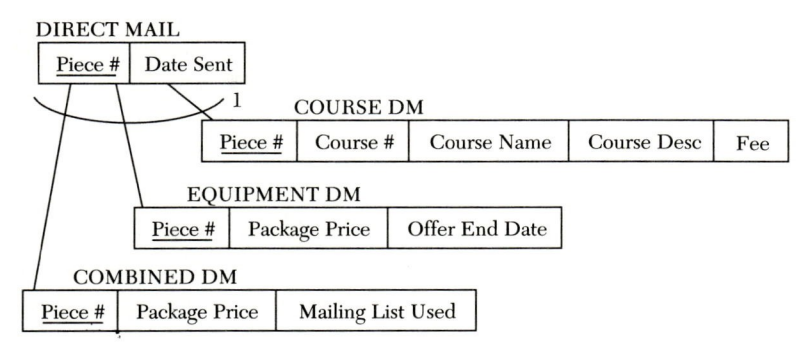

Piece #	Package Price	Mailing List Used

Answer Diagram #4

6. (a) Yes
   (b) Yes
   (c) 6

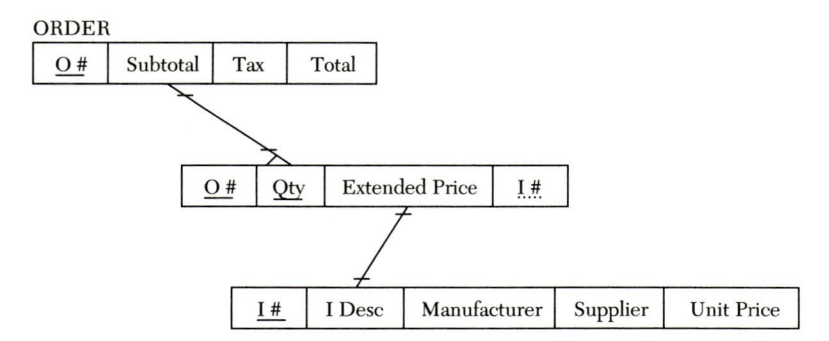

ORDER

O #	Subtotal	Tax	Total

O #	Qty	Extended Price	I #

I #	I Desc	Manufacturer	Supplier	Unit Price

Answer Diagram #5

7. The relations are in DK/NF. A relation is in DK/NF if every constraint on the relation is a logical consequence of the definition of keys and domains, and there are no modification anomalies.

Case 5 - Answers

8.

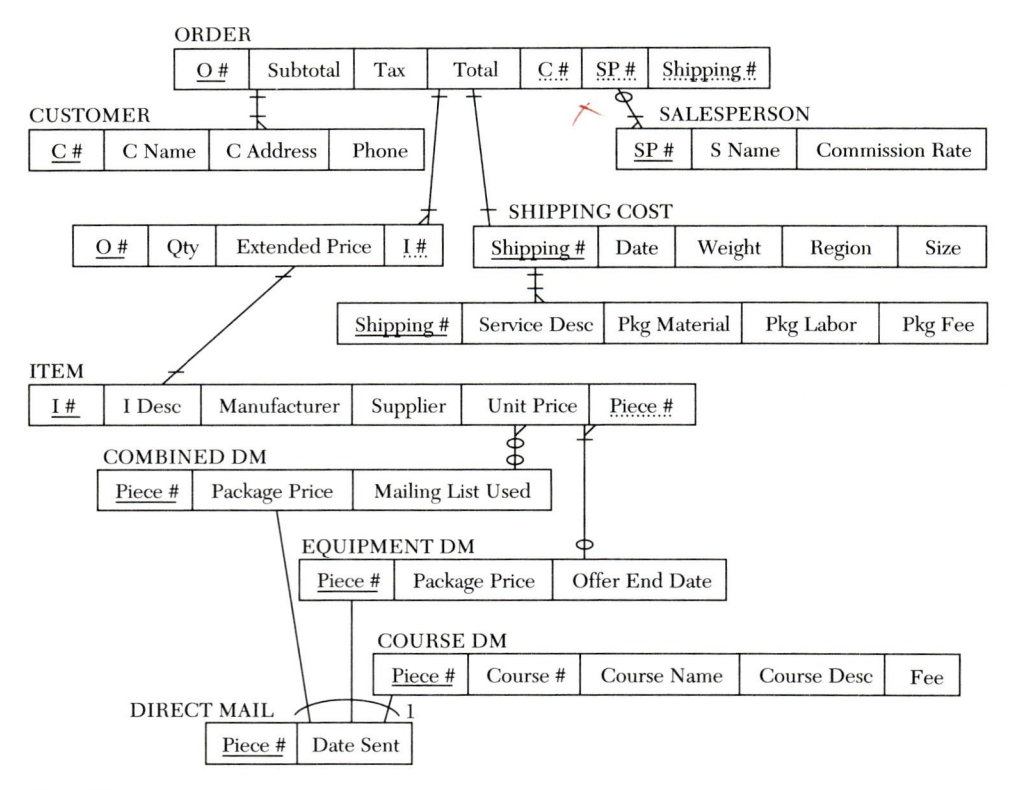

Answer Diagram #6

9. See answer for #8.

NOTE: There are no answers to Case 6.